"For anyone interested in the role of human rights in current-day Europe, the Aegean islands are a good place to start looking. They stand for some of the most flagrant human rights violations of our times, but also show the continued relevance of 'rights talk'. This book, based on thorough empirical and comparative research, contains insights on the localization of human rights with a relevance that reaches far beyond this case study. Highly recommended for policymakers and scholars alike!"

Barbara Oomen, *Professor of Sociology of Human Rights at Utrecht University and President of HZ University of Applied Sciences in Zeeland*

"Kolliniati's book creates a fruitful encounter between empirical research, political theory and jurisprudence. It shows that local actors are not passive recipients of European asylum policy, but make their voices heard in a language of rights. An extremely valuable contribution to understanding the making of human rights."

Jürgen Bast, *Professor of Public Law and European Law at Justus Liebig University Giessen, Research Group "Human Rights Discourse in Migration Societies" (MeDiMi)*

"The practical application of political philosophy is becoming increasingly important. The combination of narratives regarding human rights and asylum centers with contemporary political philosophy principles stands out as a notable innovation. Kolliniati's outstanding book adeptly navigates readers through the main arguments in the field, conducting interdisciplinary research. This is a compelling read for scholars and students interested in the subject."

George N. Politis, *Professor of Social Philosophy, National and Kapodistrian University of Athens*

"Kollinati's fascinating interdisciplinary work is a prime example of how to gain insight into complex phenomena like migration and asylum politics through a micro-oriented perspective on narratives and local actors' practices. By drawing on interviews and fieldwork in Greece, she demonstrates how human rights work in and through practices on the ground and are negotiated by various political actors using competing narratives. A must-read for students and scholars interested in narrative research, in political theory and local perspectives in IR!"

Frank Gadinger, *Professor for International Relations, University of Münster*

"A landmark contribution to both the literature on the practice of human rights and to wider debates about the future of human rights in a time of crisis, uncertainty, but also of possibility. As her beautifully written book shows, the future of human rights—as idea, as law, as politics—is in the hands of those whose lives depend upon it."

Mark Goodale, *Leverhulme Trust Visiting Professor, University of Oxford, author of Reinventing Human Rights*

Interpreting Human Rights

Kolliniati's groundbreaking book, *Interpreting Human Rights: Narratives from Asylum Centers in Greece and Philosophical Values*, challenges the notion that the interpretation and application of human rights primarily occur within the corridors of power in Strasbourg or official European institutions. It argues that such interpretation takes place in the grassroots settings of rural areas and neighborhoods, by actors who do not belong to the class of decision-making elites.

Focusing on the Aegean islands as exemplary sites of the European refugee crisis, this book draws on research conducted among local actors, including mayors, municipal councilors, representatives of NGOs and staff at refugee reception and identification centers. This book is divided into five distinctive sections: Methodology; Legal Framework and the Emergence of Hotspots; Empirical Research: Narratives of Local Actors; Local Narratives and Political Attitudes; and Glocalization of Human Rights. The study explores the role of human rights in narratives surrounding refugee flows, categorizing responses according to various political theory approaches such as global liberalism, egalitarianism, communitarianism and conservatism. By integrating applied political theory with localized human rights interpretations, this book offers actionable steps for addressing the challenges of migration in today's interconnected world.

By amplifying the voices of those directly engaged with one of contemporary Europe's most significant challenges, *Interpreting Human Rights* will appeal to scholars of sociology, political theory, politics and international law, particularly those interested in migration, human rights and refugee studies.

Maria-Artemis Kolliniati is an adjunct lecturer of Human Rights, Political Theory and Forced Migration in the MA collaborative programs at TU Darmstadt and Goethe University Frankfurt. She teaches Human Rights at the Hellenic Open University and 'Ethics, Politics, Law' at the University of Athens School of Philosophy. Previously, she taught Jurisprudence at the University of Glasgow Law School. She was awarded a scholarship from the State Scholarships Foundation (I.K.Y.) for her postdoctoral research, which she pursued and completed at the University of Athens School of Political Science. She holds a PhD in Political Science with a focus on Political Theory (2018) from the Ruprecht-Karl-University of Heidelberg.

Interpreting Human Rights

Narratives from Asylum Centers in Greece and Philosophical Values

Maria-Artemis Kolliniati

Routledge
Taylor & Francis Group
LONDON AND NEW YORK

First published 2025
by Routledge
4 Park Square, Milton Park, Abingdon, Oxon OX14 4RN

and by Routledge
605 Third Avenue, New York, NY 10158

Routledge is an imprint of the Taylor & Francis Group, an informa business

British Library Cataloguing-in-Publication Data
A catalogue record for this book is available from the British Library

ISBN: 9781032638522 (hbk)
ISBN: 9781032742052 (pbk)
ISBN: 9781003468134 (ebk)

DOI: 10.4324/9781003468134

Typeset in Times New Roman
by codeMantra

For my mother
Clio Stavrianoudaki-Kolliniati

Contents

Acknowledgments

This volume presents the refined English rendition of the Greek work titled Ανθρώπινα Δικαιώματα σε Δοκιμασία, authored by Maria-Artemis Kolliniati and published in December 2022. I extend my heartfelt thanks to my esteemed publishers, Giorgos Dardanos and Costas Dardanos, whose unwavering support and expert facilitation made the realization of the English edition seamlessly achievable. Their invaluable contributions are deeply appreciated, and I am profoundly grateful to them. Moreover, I thank the Greek State Scholarship Foundation (IKY) for awarding a scholarship for the years 2020–2022, after a stiff competitive procedure, to support my postdoctoral research that has been materialized in this book. The implementation of the postdoctoral research was co-financed by Greece and the European Union (European Social Fund) through the Operational Program 'Human Resource Development, Education and Lifelong Learning', within the framework of the Act 'Assistance of Post-Doctoral Researchers – Cycle B' (MIS 5033021), implemented by the Greek State Scholarship Foundation (IKY). The funders had no role in study design, data collection and analysis, decision to publish or preparation of the manuscript. Furthermore, I extend sincere thanks to all those instrumental in the creation of this book; their indispensable support has played a pivotal role in its fruition. Nikos-Komninos Hlepas, who supervised the postdoctoral research that led to this book; our collaboration over the years, even before the postdoc, served as inspiration for studying the local level and human rights, opening new questions reflected in this book. Despite his busy schedule and increased obligations, he always devoted time to read this study at all stages, providing continuous detailed feedback, comments, relevant literature and promptly responding whenever I needed assistance. Even though he had some disagreements with my approach at certain junctures in this book, he staunchly upholds my right to express my beliefs, even when they differ from his own, thus exemplifying his commitment to the practical application of freedom of expression. Yiannis Psycharis, for his crucial assistance, valuable guidance and encouragement to continue. Certainly, this research would not have started without his encouragement. Frank Gadinger, for the precious time he dedicated to discussing in detail the methodological framework of my research and providing guidance on narrative approach. He supported me with literature and always promptly responded to my questions. George N. Politis, amidst his demanding commitments, graciously dedicated time to peruse segments of my book, offering invaluable insights. I am deeply grateful for the lessons he consistently imparts through our collaboration and his unwavering readiness to provide guidance whenever sought. Alkis Gounaris for the time he dedicated to reading part of my study. All those who participated in this research by granting me interviews. Without their contribution, it would not have been possible to realize this research work. I hope I have satisfactorily utilized our discussions, clearly reflecting their approaches and certainly have not unjustly treated any of them. My students from TU Darmstadt and Goethe University Frankfurt who participated in the Human Rights and Forced Migration course for what they taught me through their ideas and quests. My sister Despina-Daisy for her unwavering and immediate assistance whenever I need it, as well as for sharing her scientific knowledge. Philipp, alongside our daughters Eleftheria and Clio, imbue my existence with fortitude and imbue each moment with renewed significance. Moreover, my gratitude extends to the nurturing kindergarten educators who safeguard the well-being of our cherished little ones. This book is dedicated to my mom, Clio, who's been my rock through thick and thin. I aspire to one day emulate her example by championing justice and extending aid to those in need, and to marginalized communities.

Introduction

Introduction

In Dali's painting 'Enchanted Beach with Three Fluid Graces' (1938), which adorns the cover of the Greek edition (Kolliniati 2022) of this book, the Three Graces or the Three Fates (Moirai) are depicted in a contemplative state against the backdrop of a captivating beachscape. These figures symbolize ideal beauty, joy and allure, evoking a sense of enchantment. Alternatively, in an interpretative narrative, the trio of the Three Fates holds sway over the destinies of mortals, intricately weaving the fabric of their lives from inception to inevitable conclusion. The coastal landscapes of the islands under scrutiny seamlessly integrate with the concept of enchanted beaches, acting as the initial points of arrival for desperate individuals – asylum seekers – who cling to a last vestige of hope, unaware of the unfolding of their destinies within these insular realms.

The allure of pristine beaches, the cerulean waters of the Aegean and picturesque sunsets are symbiotically linked to an ostensibly carefree existence on a Greek island, characterized by the indulgence in fresh seafood harvested from the Aegean Pelagos. However, beneath the veneer of breathtaking landscapes and promising islands lies the stark reality of isoboxes and dispersed tent settlements amidst the fields, juxtaposed with the distressing presence of lifeless bodies submerged in the sea. Across the five islands investigated in this research, a spectrum of 'enchanted beach' dimensions unfolds, interwoven with narratives from diverse actors who, whether consciously or unconsciously, use 'vernacularized' human rights discourse to address challenges associated with asylum centers.

The research places significant emphasis on 'vernacularized' human rights, as it recognizes that the interpretation and formation of human rights occur not within the confines of Strasbourg's institutions, university auditoriums or EU debates, but rather in rural communities and neighborhoods, driven by individuals outside the decision-making elite. The philosophy of rights and the practice of human rights are relational concepts. The most important theorists of human rights are neither academics nor judges – they are actors who are working at the field, politicians of the countryside, rural intellectuals and village activists (Goodale 2007, pp. 36–38).

In this context, the book focuses on the narratives of local actors regarding human rights within the Reception and Identification Centers (RICs) for asylum

DOI: 10.4324/9781003468134-1

seekers. These narratives emerge from interviews conducted with actors active on five Greek islands, specifically Chios, Cos, Leros, Lesvos and Samos. Human rights, in this study, are primarily examined at the local level, particularly within the island hotspots, thus embracing the '*glocalization*' of human rights. The increasing academic and political interest in promoting human rights at the sub-national level in Europe stems from the proximity of regional and local authorities to their constituents. Consequently, RICs and asylum seekers are closely tied to the local level due to their prolonged stay on the islands, a result of the 'geographical limitation' implemented in 2016 following the EU–Turkey joint statement. Asylum seekers reside within island communities, interacting with elected municipal officials and local actors, rather than with those making critical decisions at the national and European levels.

In the context of the 'Hotspot approach' in Greece and the 'geographical limitation' in the Aegean islands, the Greek islands have turned into places where the human rights of asylum seekers are claimed, while in some cases, they are violated. Adopting this framework, it was investigated through empirical research, what is the narrative of some local actors about the role of human rights in the context of the specific islands – hotspots – during the period from 2015 to the beginning of 2021.

In examining this research question, interviews were conducted to explore how human rights are integrated into the narratives of local actors as they interact with asylum centers in their respective areas. The study presents the results of interviews with a total of 28 actors, including elected politicians in local island governments (mayors and municipal councilors), as well as professionals and solidarity volunteers working in the field. To achieve the objectives, local actors were asked to articulate their narratives on the primary challenges within RICs and hotspot islands from 2015 to the beginning of 2021. The interviews, predominantly conducted in 2021 with supplementary sessions in 2020, constituted the primary data collection phase. The empirical findings highlight the emphasis placed by local actors on two main themes: (a) the rights and interests of local community residents and (b) the human rights of asylum seekers. Notably, the study reveals that narratives concerning concepts such as 'national sovereignty', 'local economy', 'local interest' and 'public safety of the local community' often prioritize the rights of local residents, while implicitly or explicitly overlooking the human rights of asylum seekers.

The narrative approach served as a methodological framework in two distinct ways. First, the challenges articulated by the actors in the field were interpreted through the lens of legal vocabulary, specifically in terms of potential violations of human rights law (Frankenberg 2014, p. 51), despite the actors' lack of explicit reference to rights violations. Second, the metaphors and myths that emerged within the narratives of local actors were analyzed (Gadinger et al. 2019; Freistein et al. 2020; Smith Ochoa et al. 2020) to identify the human rights violations to which these myths and metaphors alluded.

In one of the final parts of the book, the narratives of local actors are categorized into different normative frameworks based on the principles they espouse and the rights they advocate. Local actors whose narratives emphasize the prioritization of the rights and interests of members of the local society over those of asylum seekers align with partiality and theoretical frameworks such as communitarianism or conservatism. Conversely, local actors who regard the rights of citizens and asylum seekers as equally important, with a focus on highlighting violations of asylum seekers' rights, fall into the category of impartiality, aligning with theoretical frameworks such as global liberalism or egalitarianism.

Part 1

Methodology

To understand the role of human rights in Reception and Identification Centers (RICs) on Aegean islands, interviews were conducted with local actors. These interviews aimed to reveal if human rights were part of their narratives and to identify which specific rights were mentioned. This book translates these narratives into legal principles from the European Convention on Human Rights and the 1951 Refugee Convention and its 1967 Protocol. It adopts a 'practice of human rights' approach, considering how nonelites conceptualize human rights, challenging elite interpretations. Additionally, the methodology of this book also aligns with de Shalit's perspective on political theory. De Shalit (2018) argued for a distinction between cities and states in political theory, emphasizing that cities bear the brunt of immigration challenges. This recognition underscores the focus on understanding the local dynamics and challenges faced by cities and municipalities, especially in the context of immigration and asylum policies, while the normative questions are differentiated when someone focuses on the local level, instead of the state level. Interviews with 28 local actors were conducted, using a questionnaire based on the approach of Oomen and Baumgärtel (2018). Narratives and metaphors are analyzed to understand moral judgments and how individuals perceive the situation in RICs. These narratives shape understanding and reflect cultural influences and political norms on the discourse of human rights.

The main idea surrounding this book is 'vernacularized' human rights and that in recent years, there has been increasing interest in promoting human rights at the subnational level in Europe, recognizing the impact of regional and local authorities on daily life. Studies have explored the implementation of human rights at the local level. Cities and towns are seen, in political science, as agents capable of shaping interpretations of human rights, and legally, they are considered actors with rights and obligations under international law. Sociological perspectives depict cities as dynamic arenas where various actors engage in human rights discourse. Research has also examined the concept of 'vernacularization' of human rights, highlighting the integration of human rights into everyday life. Despite the growing influence of local governments, international law continues to prioritize the concept of the sovereign state. The Aegean islands serve as a focal point for refugee flows, raising questions about the role and influence of local authorities in addressing human rights issues.

DOI: 10.4324/9781003468134-2

1 Human rights and local level

In recent years, there has been a noticeable surge in academic and political interest regarding the promotion of human rights at the subnational level in Europe. This heightened attention is driven by the recognition of regional and local authorities' proximity to residents and their significant impact on the daily lives of those within their territories. Consequently, there is a growing need to delineate specific human rights obligations for subnational authorities in practical terms. For instance, the Congress of Local and Regional Authorities of the Council of Europe conducted a recent study examining the implementation of human rights at the local level (Congress of Local and Regional Authorities 2018). In 2018, it published a handbook on human rights that explored the rights of vulnerable groups, including migrants and asylum seekers, and identified 65 good practices applied in more than 25 countries.

From the perspective of political science, cities and towns are regarded as *agents* capable of providing unique interpretations of human rights. Local authorities may function as entities that shape and introduce their own perceptions of human rights in discussions and negotiations conducted at the national, regional or international level, as well as within networks of cities or municipalities. Legally, cities and towns are viewed as *actors* with the capacity to claim subjectivity under international law. Consequently, they possess the ability to assert rights and bear obligations in accordance with provisions of international law. Sociological approaches underscore the heterogeneous nature of local authorities. In sociology, cities and towns are depicted as *arenas* where various institutions, organizations and individuals are active participants, contributing to the diversification or 'pluralization' of human rights (Oomen and Durmus 2019, pp. 146–147). The existing literature has looked at the link between human rights and local government from several perspectives (de Feyter 2011). There is a growing interest in exploring a 'translocality' of human rights, challenging the traditional notion of their universality (Goodale 2022). Other studies delve into the arrival cities (Saunders 2010; Taubenböck 2018) and sanctuary cities (Darling 2009; Baumgärtel and Oomen 2019; Roy 2019), the invocation of international human rights law by local authorities to defend 'irregular' migrants (Baumgärtel and Oomen 2019) and the role of local governments and a plural understanding of human rights (Oomen and Durmus 2019), at the broader topic of refugees and the city (Sanyal 2012; Hatziprokopiou et al. 2016; Tsavdaroglou 2019), at EU migration policies and the boundaries of human rights (Bast et al. 2022),

DOI: 10.4324/9781003468134-3

at cities and migration governance (Çaglar and Schiller 2018), at hotspots for asylum seekers in Greece (Dimitriadi 2017), at hotspots and rights using critical theory as framework (Trubeta 2015), at the relationship of political and space distinguishing between state and local level ('polis') (Arendt 2018), at the topic of politics from the perspective of the city instead of the perspective of the state (Magnusson 2011; Amin and Thrift 2016) or at the 'glocalization' of human rights and cities as international agents in migration policy (Stürner and Bendel 2019) or approaches that refer to 'human rightism' characterizing mainly human rights activists as 'human rightists' (Pellet 2000). In the Aegean region, there exists a field research project aimed at investigating the operational dynamics of the hotspot system on the border islands of Greece. The study aims to discern the implications and repercussions of this system on the lives of individuals subjected to its governance, spanning the period from 2015 to 2020 (Spathopoulou 2022). There is also research on cities or on 'tiny hamlets and boroughs' or in general on the closest level to citizens (Oomen and Durmus 2019, p. 144) that formulate their policies according to human rights norms (Grigolo 2016, p. 277; Oomen 2016, p. 1). Research exists on instances where local authorities invoke international human rights law, deviating from national policies (Baumgärtel and Oomen 2019, p. 173), as well as studies focusing on the concept of 'human rights cities'. In this context, there is research on human rights cities, such as Barcelona (Grigolo 2017) or Utrecht (Oomen and van den Berg 2014). For example, the municipality of Utrecht, invoking international law and human rights provisions, has implemented policies that support the needs of undocumented migrants and those who have received negative decisions on asylum claim applications (see Oomen and van den Berg 2014; Miellet 2019, p. 215).

Moreover, in academic research, the question about the meaning of human rights to be localized in everyday spaces has been posed (see Miellet 2019, p. 214). Human rights scholars examine the local turn in human rights, exploring the concept of 'vernacularization'. This concept is exemplified by Eleanor Roosevelt, who, on the 10th anniversary of the Universal Declaration of Human Rights, emphasized the integration of human rights into everyday life (Levitt and Merry 2009, p. 441). Academics focusing on human rights delve into the concept of 'vernacularization', which denotes the 'local turn' of human rights. They explore the ways and processes adopted and adapted locally in various parts of the world, encompassing ideas and strategies that have been developed globally (Levitt and Merry 2009, p. 441). These studies challenge the rigid dichotomy between 'global' and 'local' perspectives on human rights, highlighting the diverse roles played by various actors. As noted by Sally Merry (2006), these actors encompass a wide range of individuals, including local activists, human rights lawyers, feminists, NGO leaders, academics and many others, who straddle the divide between the international community and their local contexts or 'who have one foot in the international community and the other at home' (Merry 2006, p. 42). In her study of translocal internationalism, Judith Resnik broadens this framework to encompass municipal actors, including mayors and members of city councils, who, as popularly elected officials, engage in international agreements and discussions pertaining to the defense of human rights (Resnik 2007, p. 50). However, despite the significant expansion of human rights applications, involving actors from diverse environments and governance levels, the spatial dimensions of local actors' practices in human rights remain relatively underexplored (Miellet 2019, pp. 214–215).

This book builds upon the above-mentioned scholars, particularly focusing on Oomen's approach to human rights and cities, as well as de Shalit's examination of immigration within the context of the local level (city). According to de Shalit (2018), there is a dearth of research in political theory regarding migration at the local level that clearly delineates between cities and states and this gap is critical. As de Shalit (2018) contends, when research centers on cities as destinations rather than states, it alters the moral questions surrounding migration. Therefore, political theory should distinguish between cities and states, as 'nearly all immigrants end up in cities, indeed metropolitan cities, hence it is the city rather than the state that copes with the influx of immigrants' (de Shalit 2018, p. 1–2). In fact, after the implementation of the 'hotspot approach' public policy (Neville et al. 2016; Papoutsi et al. 2019), the asylum seekers who reach one of the Aegean islands cannot move to metropolitan cities, but they do end up in port cities or small villages at Greek islands until the final adjudication of their application (in many cases even up to nine months). Thus, it becomes apparent from the hotspots that it is the islands and their inhabitants, rather than the state, who deal with the consequences of the flow of migrants in their everyday lives. The islands in the North and Southeastern Aegean have to cope with human rights claims of asylum seekers. In this context, the narratives of local actors about human rights are shaped by the existence of the Reception and Identification Centers (RICs) in their society, and different human rights violations are identified by local actors.

The responsibilities of local government, on a moral level, to protect the human rights of asylum seekers, as well as the limitations placed by the principle of non-refoulement not only on the sovereignty of the state but also on the jurisdiction of municipalities and regions, create a 'governance debate', as refugee status and regional status may be in conflict (Jones 2013, p. 77). According to Oomen and Baumgärtel (2018) local actors claim and gradually win 'key roles' in the application of the rules of international law and this can be confirmed by 'human rights cities'. Local authorities are seen as having 'increasing influence' and 'confidence' in global governance, despite the fact that international law ignores the dynamics of the local level and instead of incorporating local authorities as actors of international law, continues to adhere to the concept of 'sovereign state' (Oomen and Baumgärtel 2018). The growing power of local government is evident in the actions of local authorities. For example, the mayors of New York, London (see *#Londonisopen* campaign) and Paris, in 2016 during the United Nations Summit on Refugees and Migrants, stated through the *New York Times* that the cities would be among the first to assist those forced to flee their homelands due to violence or persecution (see De Blasio et al. 2016, as cited in Barbara Oomen and Moritz Baumgärtel, 2018, p. 608).

However, in Europe, during the same period, the 'geographic restriction' had already started to be applied since March 2016, after the EU-Turkey Agreement.

Asylum seekers until the asylum procedures were completed were obliged to be held in centers on five Greek islands in the Aegean, certainly less economically strong and less well-known than the cities of London, Paris or New York. At the same time, the Aegean islands are a gateway for a large number of refugees, while the local authorities not only did not have an 'increasing influence' about refugee decisions but in some cases, it was decided to create RICs despite the objections of the local authorities and the municipal council of the cities of the islands.

2 Empirical research

Methodology and theoretical framework

To 'translate' the narratives of local actors into legal terminology and identify potential human rights violations in their accounts, interviews were conducted with local actors from the Aegean islands. Participants were asked about their perspectives on the primary challenges faced by Reception and Identification Centers (RICs) and hotspot islands due to the presence of RICs. The research aimed to ascertain whether human rights featured in the narratives of local actors and if so, which specific human rights were explicitly or implicitly referenced. Additionally, the questions regarding challenges aimed to determine whether the narratives of local actors (Heinelt and Terizakis 2020; Hlepas and Koliastasis 2021) primarily focused on the human rights of asylum seekers, the human rights of islanders or if human rights did not feature prominently in their perspectives.

In the next section of this work, initially, the narratives of the local actors will be presented[1] in detail for each Aegean island, where the RICs are located. The narratives cover the approaches of elected officials, such as mayors and municipal councilors, as well as those of activists and employees in NGOs and international organizations working on the islands. Interviews conducted with local actors have been translated into the legal principles and rights (Schaffer and Smith 2004; McCrudden 2006; UNDP 2009; United Nations Human Rights 2012; Saibih 2019) of the European Convention on Human Rights and the 1951 Refugee Convention. This book is the result of research based on the 'practice of human rights' approach which concerns the different ways in which social actors approach the idea of human rights and their various forms. In this approach, actors may talk about human rights or criticize the idea of human rights and ultimately may 'enact' human rights by talking about them in a simple/'folk' way using colloquialism or by referring to legal concepts (Goodale 2007, p. 36). This book draws on Goodale's approach, assuming that nonelites – such as rural intellectuals, village activists, civil servants, rural politicians and municipal councilors – all of them, in many cases, are important human rights theorists. Hence, the idea of human rights is shaped and conceptualized by these rural and local actors, i.e., outside the 'discourse of elites' and away from elite interpretations of rights. Therefore, the separation between 'philosophy' of rights and 'practice' of rights is misleading (Goodale 2007, p. 38) because the philosophy of human rights is directly intertwined with their practice, as it is shaped by local actors.

DOI: 10.4324/9781003468134-4

In this context, interviews were conducted (Reed and Padskocimaite 2012) with 28 local actors active in the field on the islands of settlement of the RICs for asylum seekers. To develop a questionnaire and codify the responses in MAXQDA, some elements of Oomen and van den Berg's (2014) approach were adopted, according to which local actors can share four human rights positions: (a) explicitly invoke human rights and their obligations; (b) implicitly invoke them (e.g., using alternative terminology); (c) explicitly ignore human rights and obligations because they disagree with their content and (d) implicitly ignore the obligations that human rights entail, due to a lack of knowledge regarding their existence. Furthermore, narratives and metaphors serve as crucial analytical categories in this book. Narratives play a vital role in understanding a problem, as they provide a clear framing of moral elements. They articulate how individuals describe the situation, particularly concerning the RICs. Through these descriptions, fundamental categories emerge, delineating who is deemed 'guilty' and who is 'accused', all reflecting moral judgments inherent in the narratives. The narratives individuals share are influenced by both the realm of possibility and the cultural significance within their context (Patterson and Monroe 1998, pp. 320, 324–326). It is essential to underscore that narratives are never neutral; rather, they strive to 'make sense of the world', a crucial aspect of this study (Patterson and Monroe 1998, p. 316).

Note

1 The final results of the research were presented on 3 November 2022 at the online conference Crisis and Forced Migration: Manifestations of power in a changing world (CARFMS22) organized from 2–4 November 2022 by York University – Center for Refugee Studies, Canada – Toronto, Ontario (in collaboration with the Human Rights Program of St Paul's University College, University of Waterloo). Moreover, this study has been presented at colloquia at the TU Darmstadt Institute of Political Science and the Justus-Liebig-Universität Gießen Institute of Political Science.

Part 2

Legal framework and the emergence of hotspots

The intricate legal framework surrounding the protection of asylum seekers is related by key instruments such as the 1951 Geneva Refugee Convention, the Universal Declaration of Human Rights and the Common European Asylum System. Through a meticulous analysis, this part explores the evolving interpretation of refugee rights, with a particular focus on the principle of nonrefoulement and procedural guarantees delineated in directives like Directive 2013/32/EU. Additionally, the Schengen Borders Code and relevant case law are examined to illuminate both the challenges and advancements in safeguarding refugee rights within the European context. Furthermore, this part provides a detailed examination of Greece's legal framework concerning asylum seekers, shedding light on regulations governing the involvement of nongovernmental organizations in rescue operations and the obligations of individuals to aid. Through a thorough exploration of these legal provisions and their practical implications, this part underscores the delicate balance between humanitarian imperatives and legal constraints in ensuring the protection of asylum seekers within Greece's borders.

Moreover, this chapter delves into the role played by the European Union in managing migration flows through the establishment and management of hotspots, particularly on the Greek islands. It traces the genesis and evolution of these hotspots within the EU framework, highlighting the differing interpretations of the term and the significant influence of the Mediterranean migration crisis. In this context, the establishment of Reception and Identification Centers aimed at efficiently processing arrivals, yet their effectiveness dwindled as refugee flows surged, leading to a myriad of human rights challenges. Over time, these hotspots transitioned from transit points to semipermanent residences, exacerbating issues such as overcrowding and inadequate infrastructure. Delays in asylum procedures, coupled with geographical restrictions, further strained resources and led to overpopulation. Additionally, this chapter explores how the COVID-19 pandemic and strained Greek–Turkish relations exacerbated the challenges faced by hotspot communities. In summary, this chapter provides a comprehensive exploration of the multifaceted dynamics shaping migration governance in the EU, encompassing legal frameworks, hotspot management and the intricate balance between humanitarian needs and legal obligations. Through its thorough analysis, this chapter sheds light on the complexities inherent in addressing migration challenges and underscores the imperative of finding sustainable and rights-respecting solutions within the European context.

DOI: 10.4324/9781003468134-5

3 EU and national legal provisions about asylum seekers

Several pivotal legal instruments establish the foundational framework for safeguarding the rights of asylum seekers. These include the 1951 Geneva Refugee Convention and its 1967 Protocol, the Universal Declaration of Human Rights (UDHR), the Common European Asylum System (CEAS), the Directive 2013/32/EU delineating common procedures for granting and withdrawing international protection, the Directive on Asylum Procedures (Directive 2013/32/EU), the Schengen Borders Code embodied in Regulation (EU) 2016/399 and the pertinent elements within the Greek legal framework.

In delineating the legal foundation for safeguarding the rights of asylum seekers, the 1951 Geneva Refugee Convention assumes a paramount role. Specifically, the convention confers refugee status upon individuals confronting persecution based on political beliefs, race, religion or nationality. Its primary emphasis lies in shielding those with a 'well-founded fear of persecution' due to factors including race, religion, nationality, membership in a particular social group or political opinion. While serving as a cornerstone in refugee protection, the convention's definition of persecution is inherently circumscribed, potentially leaving certain situations leading to forced displacement, such as those arising from general violence, war or environmental factors, outside its explicit purview. It is imperative to acknowledge that the interpretation and application of the convention have undergone evolution over time. In response, various international discussions and agreements have transpired, seeking to address the protection needs of individuals compelled to flee due to armed conflicts, violence or environmental disasters. Advocates posit the necessity for a more expansive conception of refugee status to encompass these nuanced circumstances. Notwithstanding the rigorous limitations intrinsic to the demarcation of 'persecution' as articulated in the 1951 Geneva Refugee Convention, rendering it inadequate in encompassing diverse scenarios necessitating international safeguarding, such as those involving environmental or even war refugees, the convention endures as an indispensable legal framework providing essential protection.

Notably, Article 33 of the Geneva Convention solidifies the 'principle of non-refoulement', underscoring the prohibition of returning individuals to locations where their life or freedom may be endangered. In accordance with Article 31 of the 1951 Refugee Convention, the states that are parties to this international

DOI: 10.4324/9781003468134-6

agreement are prohibited from enforcing its regulations to penalize refugees from a third country solely on the grounds of their illegal entry or presence within their territory. The stipulations of Article 31 elucidate this principle by emphasizing that refugees, who directly arrive from a region where their life or freedom was under threat as defined by Article 1, shall not be subjected to penalties for unauthorized entry or presence, provided they promptly present themselves to the authorities and provide compelling reasons for their irregular entry or presence. Moreover, the contracting states are obligated to refrain from imposing restrictions on the movements of such refugees, beyond what is deemed necessary. These restrictions are only permissible until the refugee's status in the country is regularized or until they secure admission into another country. Importantly, the contracting states are mandated to afford such refugees a reasonable timeframe and all essential facilities to secure admission into an alternative country (Article 31 of the 1951 Refugee Convention). This underscores the humanitarian principles embedded within the 1951 Refugee Convention.

Additionally, the UDHR contributes significantly, particularly through Article 14. This provision explicitly acknowledges the right to seek and enjoy asylum from persecution, coupled with outlined restrictions. In further elucidating this legal milieu, one must consider the inclusion of the 1969 Vienna Convention on the Law of Treaties (VCLT). The VCLT introduces a nuanced approach to treaty interpretation, emphasizing values such as good faith, along with a consideration of the objects and purposes of a treaty (Art. 31(1) and Art. 31(3) 1969 VCLT). In this context, the interpretation of terms within the 1951 Geneva Refugee Convention and 1967 Protocol, such as 'persecution', 'expel' or 'return', is intricately tied to these foundational values and principles. Thus, their interpretation must consider the overarching objectives and aspirations of international law.

In alignment with prevailing legal norms and principles, the legal framework of the European Union, as illustrated by entities like the CEAS, represents an institutional structure guided by the directives set forth in the Directive 2011/95/EU (EU Qualification Directive). This directive, with meticulous attention, delineates the parameters of asylum, particularly within the purview of Articles 9–10, where the comprehensive definition of acts of persecution and the underlying reasons for persecution are articulated. Relevant provisions are the Dublin Convention which entered into force in 1997 and concerns the practice of submitting an asylum claim to the first safe country of entry ('first point of entry'). The Dublin Convention, which ceased its validity on 16/03/2003, underwent revision in 2003 and has since been supplanted by Regulation (EU) No 604/2013, commonly referred to as the Dublin III Regulation. This regulation, enacted on 26 June 2013, has subsequently undergone amendments, incorporating an exception to the 'country of first entry' rule. Article 17 of the Dublin III Regulation states that the exception to the 'first point of entry' rule can be triggered to reunite family members, relatives or persons linked by any other type of family relationship. Article 18, par. 1 (a) of the Dublin III Regulation contains provisions regarding the obligations of the responsible member state to 'take charge' request for reasons of family reunification, despite the fact that the Member State may not be a 'first country of entry' (see Regulation (EU) No 604/2013). The current Dublin regulation will be replaced by April 2024, by the Asylum and Migration Management Regulation (AMMR).

Moreover, Directive 2013/32/EU, commonly referred to as the Directive on Asylum Procedures, guarantees the right to apply for asylum at the borders of a state. In the Directive 2013/32/EU, the requirements for the procedures for 'withdrawal of international protection' are determined and a progressive interpretation of the principle of nonrefoulement of the Geneva Convention is given. To delve into greater detail, the plea for asylum at a state's border, as outlined by the Geneva Convention, initially underwent a conservative interpretation. According to the conservative reading of the Convention at the time of its adoption, the principle of nonrefoulement was deemed inapplicable to those positioned at a state's borders who had not yet crossed into its territory, or, in other words, who were not effectively eluding the scrutiny of border guards (Robinson 1953, p. 163; Grahl-Madsen 1963; as cited in Carens 2013, p. 12). However, when subjected to legal scrutiny, this approach proves contentious, as individuals possess the entitlement to seek international protection at a nation's borders, regardless of their physical presence within the sovereign territory of that state. In this context, a more progressive interpretation of the nonrefoulement principle aligns with the provisions of Directive 2013/32/EU. This directive, aiming to harmonize asylum procedures across Europe, unequivocally safeguards the right to seek asylum at a state's borders.

Article 3, paragraph 1, of the Directive on Asylum Procedures (Directive 2013/32/EU) outlines the expansive applicability of the Directive, asserting that it is pertinent to all applications for international protection initiated within the territory, including at borders, in territorial waters or transit zones of the member states. This jurisdiction extends to cover the withdrawal of international protection as well. Furthermore, Article 9, paragraph 1, within the same Directive affirms the entitlement of asylum seekers to remain within the member state where they have submitted their asylum request until the completion of the asylum examination procedure. Notably, none of the provisions contained therein allows for any derogation from these established rights. The absence or submission of counterfeit documents, when adequately substantiated by the concerned party, should not trigger the application of a border or expedited procedure. Precisely, as delineated within its stipulations, Directive 2013/32/EU asserts that, contingent upon the applicant's ability to substantiate a valid cause, the absence of entry documents or the utilization of counterfeit documentation should not inherently trigger an automatic resort to border or expedited procedures (Regulation (EU) 2016/399, introduction, par. 21). In consonance with Directive 2013/32/EU, which safeguards the entitlement to seek asylum at a state's borders, the Greek Law 4939/2022, specifically articulated in Article 95, delineates provisions governing the submission of applications for international protection at the borders and transit zones of the nation's ports or airports.

Furthermore, the Schengen Borders Code, specifically Regulation (EU) 2016/399, underscores in its provisions that migration and the traversal of external borders by a substantial number of third-country nationals should not inherently be perceived as a threat to public policy or internal security (Regulation (EU) 2016/399, introduction, par. 26). Concurrently, the Schengen Borders Code governs the movement of individuals across both internal and external borders of member states. This regulatory framework explicitly safeguards the rights of refugees and those seeking international protection, emphasizing the principle of nonrefoulement (Regulation (EU) 2016/399, Article 3, par. b). Pertinent considerations include the precedent case law of the Court of Justice of the European Union, Article 8 of the European Convention on Human Rights (ECHR) enshrining respect for private and family life and specifically defining the concept of 'family', along with Article 4 of Protocol No. 4 of the ECHR prohibiting the collective expulsion of aliens. In cases related to asylum requests and deportations, Article 3 of the ECHR (absolute right) is often applied, referencing the prohibition of torture or inhuman or degrading treatment or punishment (see *D v. UK* in ECtHR case law at Kolliniati 2019, p). However, a significant decision by the European Court of Human Rights (ECtHR), which has been extensively scrutinized by both academic and practitioner circles, pertains to the case of *ND and NT vs. Spain* (Grand Chamber, judgment of 13 February 2020). In this verdict, the ECtHR determined that the deportations under consideration were characterized as 'expulsions' yet did not meet the criteria for being deemed 'collective' in nature. The adjudication rendered by the ECtHR in the matter of *ND and NT vs. Spain* has been construed as endorsing, if not tacitly condoning, pushback practice of Spain. This discernment is widely regarded as a substantive regression with profound implications for the safeguarding of rights pertaining to refugees and migrants (see European Center for Constitutional and Human Rights 2020). The judgment, in effect, is perceived as a notable setback in the ongoing discourse surrounding the protection and enforcement of the rights of individuals within the purview of refugee and migrant categories.

In practice, the protection of asylum seekers is a complex matter, extending beyond the strict legal provisions governing asylum applications. The legal framework concerning rescue scenarios becomes of paramount significance in this context, prompting the fundamental question of whether an entity possesses the right and/or responsibility to provide assistance to an individual in distress within the territorial waters of Greece. More precisely, within the framework of Greek legislation, the Ministerial Decision No. 3063/2020 and the Ministerial Decision No. 10616/2020 intricately delineate the operational parameters of the 'Register of Greek and Foreign Non-Governmental Organizations (NGOs)' and the 'Register of Members of Non-Governmental Organizations (NGOs)'. These registers specifically pertain to entities engaged in issues about international protection, immigration and social integration within the sovereign confines of the Greek Territory. The primary objective of the Registry is the meticulous documentation of individuals who come into contact with asylum seekers, with a particular emphasis on vulnerable demographics such as women, minors and unaccompanied minors. This scrutiny extends to individuals possessing unbridled access to and active involvement in Reception and Identification Centers (RICs) and other facilities dedicated to hosting asylum seekers. The overarching aim is to institute a discerning exclusionary criterion, preventing individuals with a history of delinquent behavior or criminal convictions from engaging in direct contact with asylum seekers and those under international protection, thereby aligning with the broader pursuit of public interest. The ramifications of these regulatory provisions reverberate notably within the RICs established on Greek islands. Following the implementation of these legal measures, exclusive access to these facilities was accorded solely to NGOs that had successfully registered in the prescribed Registry. This select group of registered NGOs became eligible to enter RICs and extend their services and aid to asylum seekers, reflecting a paradigm shift directly shaped by the delineated legal framework.

Furthermore, the legislative framework within Greece, pertinent to the discourse on human rights and asylum centers situated on the Greek islands, is intricately linked to the legal mechanisms sanctioning entities to undertake the rescue of individuals in distress. In greater specificity, indigenous and international voluntary organizations, civil society entities and nongovernmental organizations (NGOs), along with their constituents, staff and affiliates, enjoy the entitlement to furnish rescue assistance within the territorial jurisdiction delineated by the Hellenic Coast Guard. This entitlement is subject to the prerequisite of collaborative engagement with Greek or foreign NGOs duly registered in the specialized NGO registry (Law 4825/2021, art. 40; Ministerial Decision No. 3063/2020; Ministerial Decision No. 10616/2020). To operate within this legal framework, these local actors must have been proactively incorporated into the Local Emergency Plans of the Port Authorities for search and rescue incidents, adhering to the directives and mandates issued by the port authorities (Law 4825/2021, Article 40, paragraph 1, b). Additionally, their involvement is sanctioned in incidents involving the 'management of irregular entry of persons by sea', provided they have secured prior written approval from the Hellenic Coast Guard authorities, preceded by informing the authorities of their intended actions when the involvement of Hellenic authorities is unfeasible (Law 4825/2021, Article 40, paragraph 1, c). Noncompliance with these provisions incurs legal consequences, with a potential 1-year prison sentence for the implicated local actors. In the event of an accident resulting from such violations during a maritime rescue operation, a more severe penalty, potentially exceeding three years of imprisonment or as dictated by relevant statutes, is enforced (Law 4825/2021, Article 40, paragraph 2). Moreover, beyond the circumscribed entitlement to act delineated by the aforementioned clauses, a legal obligation to render assistance is established. The Criminal Code stipulates that deliberate failure to rescue another from a life-threatening situation, despite possessing the capability to do so without jeopardizing one's own life or health, constitutes a punishable offense, attracting a potential imprisonment term of up to one year (see Criminal Code (Law 4619/2019) Article 307-Failure to offer assistance). Within the framework of the Greek legal system, the nuanced response to this issue delineates that individuals are permitted to extend assistance to those seeking international protection, subject to specific conditions. Concurrently, Greek law, as enshrined in the Criminal Code, imposes an obligation on individuals to render aid to those in need, provided that such assistance does not jeopardize their own safety. This dual perspective underscores the intricate balance between humanitarian considerations and legal constraints, emphasizing the imperative of aiding those in distress while maintaining due regard for formal constraints as mandated by the legal framework.

4 Hotspots mandate and the role of the EU

In the emergence of hotspots, the European Union assumed a pivotal role, thereby significantly influencing this trajectory, while its genesis has different interpretations. First, there is no universally agreed-upon definition for the term 'hotspot'; rather, the European Commission (EC) characterizes it as an 'integrated approach'. In the EC's view, this approach aims to strengthen the capacity of member states to manage crises arising from pressures at the Union's external borders (Papoutsi et al. 2019). Second, the concept of the 'Mediterranean migration crisis' appears to have played a crucial role in shaping the hotspot approach. This framing has seemingly influenced the development and implementation of policies, emphasizing the urgency and necessity of addressing migration challenges in the Mediterranean region. This framing enables the swift articulation of policies that might not have materialized within such a condensed timeframe. This is not a novel occurrence, as the construction of migration as a crisis has been observed before. This framing allows policymakers to treat migration as an exceptional condition, compelling them to seemingly 'order' the perceived 'disorder' at the border (see Jeandesboz and Pallister-Wilkins 2014, as it is cited by Papoutsi et al. 2019).

The concept of the initial Reception and Identification Centers (RICs) originated in 2011 under Law 3907/2011, subsequently evolving into their present structure with the European Agenda on Migration COM/2015/0240 and the Greek Ministerial Decision 2969/2015 (Government Gazette 2602/B/2.12.2015). These centers were established to oversee migration flows, with EASO, Frontex and Europol operating collaboratively to manage migrant identification, fingerprinting and registration at these locations. The introduction of the first reception center at the Greek borders was intended to promptly identify arrivals, evaluate their requirements and expedite procedures. Before this, police handled identification, a practice still observed in locations such as Rhodes and smaller islands. The inception of a border mechanism in 2013 led to the establishment of an RIC in Evros and mobile units for the first reception in Lesvos and Chios, later evolving into RICs. According to a local actor's account, the 2013 goal was to swiftly identify and record individuals reaching the border, with their stay not exceeding 25 days. Subsequently, they were either referred to other facilities or released. However, as refugee flows increased in 2014 and surged dramatically in 2015, it became evident that the centers in Chios, Lesvos and Samos were inadequate, losing their intended

DOI: 10.4324/9781003468134-7

role as stipulated by Greek law. Consequently, 1,000 of people accumulated in these centers, deviating from the initial objectives (21/01/21 P14).

During the period between 2015 and 2016, asylum seekers arriving at the designated hotspots experienced brief stays, as these centers functioned as transitional points or 'stepping stones'. Upon arriving at the island hotspots via sea routes, individuals underwent registration and security checks to establish their identity as they crossed the border into Europe. Subsequently, within 1 or 2 days, they obtained the necessary documents and proceeded inland. Consequently, residents lived in tents within olive groves, yet the population of asylum seekers in these locations varied, with different individuals accumulating over time. The transient nature of residency during this period resulted in a continuous influx and departure of asylum seekers. This temporal dynamic posed a significant challenge to the local community, as it grappled with the ever-changing composition of residents in the area. Concurrently, a noteworthy aspect was observed as a considerable number of residents demonstrated solidarity with refugees, thereby illustrating a multifaceted societal response to the dynamic circumstances.

> During that period, the pressure wasn't on asylum seekers but on local communities. In 2015, thousands arrived on islands, going from shores to the centres for registration. The influx overwhelmed the areas with many foreigners. Yet, the admirable part is how local communities hospitably received them, despite the challenges posed by the large number of arrivals.
>
> (21/01/21 P14)

In 2015, those departing the islands traversed inland, proceeding through Idomeni along the Balkan route, ultimately reaching Austria, Germany and the Nordic countries. The impetus behind the 'hotspots' policy aimed at regaining control over the prevailing situation. Consequently, negotiations transpired, culminating in the EU–Turkey joint statement in 2015 and the inception of the hotspots approach in March 2016. Subsequent to the implementation of the EU–Turkey statement and the hotspots approach, the islands ceased functioning merely as transit points for asylum seekers, barring specific exceptions; individuals were expressly prohibited from relocating inland. A pivotal determination ensued, mandating the examination of asylum requests by the Greek Asylum Service to transpire on the islands. This strategic measure was designed to activate the readmission process to Turkey should it be deemed a safe haven for Syrian asylum seekers, aligning with the provisions outlined in the EU–Turkey Agreement.

Subsequent to this juncture, a persistence of the same cohort seeking asylum manifested on the island, bereft of adequate infrastructure to accommodate their presence. Since 2016, a protracted duration of stay for asylum seekers has ensued on 'hotspots' islands, dictated by the elongated processes involved in request adjudication. With the prohibition of the relocation of asylum seekers to the inland, inherent challenges within RICs emerged, notably characterized by overcrowding, insufficient housing, compromised hygiene conditions and precarious safety conditions, particularly affecting women and children.

> In 2015, a significant shift occurred as European laws governing entry, reception and movement within the EU were largely revoked. Prior to this, individuals from third countries traveled through Greece, Idomeni and Balkan nations, reaching destinations like Austria and Germany. This movement, mainly on foot, was tolerated for months. By late 2015, Germany's border closure prompted other nations to follow suit.
>
> (26/01/21 P17)

In the challenging landscape of migration management in Greece, asylum procedures on the islands often experience delays exacerbated by the imposition of 'geographical restriction' following the EU–Turkey agreement, contributing to overpopulation. Despite the provision lacking formal documentation within the agreement, Turkey, in practice, does not accept the return of individuals who have relocated from the islands to the mainland. Complicating matters further, returns to Turkey have been suspended since March 2020 due to the global pandemic and strained Greek–Turkish relations. In the current context, Closed Controlled Access Centers (CCACs) have been established and are operational across the Greek islands. These centers have replaced the previous RICs and are located in the areas formerly occupied by the RICs, with exceptions noted on Samos, where the CCAC is situated in the Zervou Area, and on Leros, where it is located in Xirokampos. Despite local opposition, as elaborated in this book, these facilities have been established and are currently functioning on the islands. They offer increased capacity compared to the RICs and provide various inclusive services, including shops, canteens and other facilities (Ministry of Migration and Asylum).

Part 3

Empirical research

Narratives of local actors

The fact that numerous individuals risk their lives traveling to Europe from countries like Syria, Eritrea, Afghanistan and others serves as an example of the ongoing human rights violations occurring on a daily basis (Oomen, 2015, p. 506). The arrival of asylum seekers on the Aegean islands underscores these violations. However, to what extent are human rights protected when asylum seekers eventually reach the Aegean islands and approach Europe? What role do rights play and what are the main challenges associated with Reception and Identification Centers in the Aegean? According to Oomen (2015), there are two prevailing strains in the field of human rights. First, there is a need to 'bring human rights back' to their origins, particularly in Western democracies. Second, there is often growing resistance against human rights in these democracies, with academics and politicians questioning international human rights bodies such as the European Court of Human Rights (Oomen 2015, p. 507).

The need to 'bring rights back' to their origins refers to the discrepancy between the commitments of Western democracies to protect universal, inalienable or economic, social and educational rights as reflected in the international conventions they have signed and the practical implementation of these commitments, which often remains confined to paper. The establishment of Reception and Identification Centers (RICs) for asylum seekers on the Aegean islands and the imposition of a 'geographical restriction' on these islands until the completion of asylum procedures reveal violations of rights affecting various individuals. The prolonged residency of asylum seekers in these centers, along with the substandard conditions within them, not only infringes upon the human rights of those seeking asylum but also forces local communities to witness these violations, challenging the glocalization of human rights. This dual impact contributes to divisions within the local communities of the islands, fostering racist tendencies and acts.

In light of these challenges, there arises a heightened necessity to restore and safeguard human rights in Western democracies. Recognizing the pivotal role that human rights can play in societal improvement, it becomes essential to address the multifaceted repercussions emanating from RICs. In this vein, the Aegean islands inherently become arenas where the preservation or compromise of human rights comes to the forefront. Consequently, a pertinent inquiry arises: what are

DOI: 10.4324/9781003468134-8

the implications of local actors' interpretations of the role of human rights in the Aegean islands, particularly regarding the glocalization of human rights?

The challenges discussed by interviewees are contextualized within the time-frame of their respective interviews. At the time of the English publication of this book, Closed Controlled Access Centers for asylum seekers will have been constructed and operational on the islands. Throughout the field research conducted for this book, these structures have been a focal point in the discourse of local actors, with the majority expressing opposition to the operation of these closed facilities on the islands.

5 Chios, Vial

The Reception and Identification Center (RIC) designated for asylum seekers in Chios is situated in Vial at Chalkeios, an integral municipal district within the jurisdiction of the Chios municipality. Chios, comprising three municipalities, encompasses a permanent population of 26,850 inhabitants, as per the Hellenic Statistical Authority's 2011 census, with the island's total population reaching 51,320 individuals. Preceding the implementation of the Kallikratis Law, the municipal district of Chalkeios was affiliated with the municipality of Kampochoro, subsequently merging with the overarching municipality of Chios. The designated capacity of the RIC on the island officially stands at 1,014 people. However, operational figures reveal that in 2019, the facility accommodated 6,078 asylum seekers, while in 2020, the resident count was reduced to 2,693 individuals (Ministry of Immigration and Asylum, annual report 12/2020). In addition to the aforementioned RIC in Vial, Chios hosts a Hospitality Structure for refugees and asylum seekers in Souda, albeit beyond the scope of this particular research. Furthermore, the ESTIA program extends accommodation outside the RIC structure for asylum seekers belonging to vulnerable groups.

Noteworthy is the municipal leadership during the interview period (2020–2021), steered by Mayor Stamatis Karmantzis of the municipal faction 'Sympraksi Dimiourgias'. His statements regarding Europe and criticisms against the Turkish ethnic group elicited reactions and discourse in the media. The mayor of Chios is the sole mayor among the islands considered in this research who ultimately declined to provide an interview for the purposes of this specific study. The municipal council of the Chios comprises several political parties: 'Protovoulia gia ti Chio', 'Chios Brosta', 'Laiki Syspeirosi Chiou', 'Diktyo Politon Chiou' and 'Chiaki Sympoliteia', as well as two municipal councilors who transitioned to the independent status from their respective municipal parties.

Empirical research on the RIC of Vial, Chios

The RIC of Vial in Chios is situated on municipal land, originally utilized by the municipality for informal recycling activities at an old factory site. In 2015, the municipality acquired this property through a loan. The municipal authority presented a proposal to the municipal council to repurpose the land for both recycling

DOI: 10.4324/9781003468134-9

and the establishment of facilities for the RIC. While the RIC operates, the recycling plant remains inactive, with the surrounding area accommodating tents, containers, the Asylum Service, the First Reception and the High Commission.

The initial agreement with the municipal authority involved signing a contract to house the RIC in the specific area for three years, concurrently agreeing that the municipality would provide the area without charge. Local actors assert that citizens are indirectly repaying the loan for the property's purchase through municipal fees. Additionally, the original plan envisioned establishing a committee, including the mayor, the president of Chalkeios, and three members from the Ministry of Immigration, among others. This committee was intended to facilitate municipal participation in RIC decision-making. In practice, the municipality appointed its members to the committee, while the Ministry did not, resulting in the committee's inactivity (25/02/21 P20; 14/01/21 P12).

At the time of the interviews, the municipal councilors were not allowed to enter the facilities of the RIC, while there are court verdicts which state that the property should be returned to the municipality, as the concession contract for the property was for three years and expired in December 2018. According to narratives of some local actors in Chios, the refugee flows in 2015 were something unprecedented, for, such a large population movement had to take place since the Second World War. It was not the first time the islands faced refugee flows, but it was the first time they were called upon to manage such a large number of people, as there were periods when arrivals at Chios island reached around 300 people a day.

Challenges in the RIC of Chios

One of the prominent challenges identified in the RIC in Vial pertains to substantial overcrowding, surpassing the originally planned capacity (03/12/20 P8; 14/01/21 P12; 14/01/21 P13; 25/02/21 P20). This overcrowding is exacerbated by the cohabitation of individuals across diverse age groups within a confined space (14/01/21 P12; 25/02/21 P20). Within the RIC, the stipulated capacity allows for the accommodation of merely 900 individuals. Conforming to a Council of State (CoE/ΣτE) verdict, asylum seekers residing therein should not surpass the specified threshold of 1,100 individuals. Nevertheless, during the interview phase, the actual demographic within the RIC of Vial revealed a substantial overage, with approximately 3,000 asylum seekers in residence, thus exceeding the designated limit. As a consequence, a considerable number of asylum seekers are compelled to reside beyond the confines of the officially designated camp, utilizing pallets or the ground for shelter. This exposes them to a spectrum of hazards, encompassing adverse weather conditions and the absence of proper waste disposal facilities, thereby precipitating sanitary issues (14/01/21 P12; 14/01/21 P13; 03/12/20 P8). Given that asylum seekers were residing in tents situated outside the official RIC within the local fields, a pertinent query arose regarding the entity responsible for waste management and oversight of living conditions. This ambiguity resulted from the asylum seekers residing in areas beyond the officially designated structures. Consequently, a lack of accountability emerged, with neither the municipality nor the RIC administration assuming responsibility (03/12/20 P8). The conditions within the RIC in Vial have been unequivocally characterized as 'deplorable' by various actors (14/01/21 P12; 14/01/21 P13). Furthermore, concerns such as drug trafficking, sexual harassment and the abuse of women and minors within the RIC have been reported (03/12/20 P8).

Primary healthcare in Chios is deemed insufficient, initially provided by the National Public Health Organization (EOΔY, formerly KEELPNO) exclusively to vulnerable groups. Consequently, nongovernmental organizations (NGOs) were enlisted to address the primary healthcare needs of other demographic segments and Chios Hospital played a role in this endeavor (14/01/21 P12). Nonetheless, the facilities at the General Hospital of Chios were originally designed to cater to a limited population, proportionate to the island's demographic. They are now inadequate to meet the escalating healthcare demands associated with the provision of services to the immigrant population (25/02/21 P20).

> On January 7, 2021, Chios hosted 2,394 asylum seekers in the Vial RIC, designed for 1,014 people, resulting in makeshift living conditions with tents and sheds. Another 285 individuals resided in UNHCR apartments via the ESTIA program, managed by ARSIS, along with 12 minors in METAdrasis' hostel. Though officially recorded as 2,691 people, it is acknowledged that additional individuals are informally housed through the ESTIA program. Notably, there are instances of people with rejected asylum claims living in abandoned houses, vulnerable to arrest and deportation.
>
> (14/01/21 P12)

Local actors point out that an approximate expenditure of 1,000,000 euros was allocated for the construction of the RIC in Vial. Despite recommendations from municipal councilors who brought attention to specific cultural nuances of Arab individuals, such as prevalent shower usage, that warranted consideration during the RIC's construction, these inputs were reportedly disregarded by the ministry overseeing the project. Consequently, damages were reported within two months of the reception center's initial operation in February 2016.

> The Ministry consistently overlooked cultural considerations, leading to inherent problems in the construction process from the outset, compounded by issues of overpopulation.
>
> (14/01/21 P12)

A challenging aspect encompasses not only the congestion of individuals within confined spaces but also the diverse ethnic backgrounds of those residing in the RIC. Narratives reveal complications stemming from the cohabitation of conflicting ethnic and religious groups. Within such a sizable population, instances of misconduct and disruptive behavior by certain individuals have been reported (25/02/21 P20).

Challenges in Chios due to the existence of the RIC at Vial

While institutional decisions made at higher government levels directly influence human rights, there is a noticeable absence of collaboration between EU institutions and national governments with local actors in rural areas on matters concerning human rights in the Aegean. Despite the pivotal impact of these facilities on human rights within the rural locales where RICs are situated, the local level finds itself marginalized in the decision-making process. In the narrative of local actors, the main decisions regarding the RICs in the Aegean are taken mainly by the EU, while the EU «ignores which are the islands of the Aegean», since the majority of those who participate in the EU institutions «lack even a basic awareness of Chios' location on the map» (14/01/21 P12).

The residents of Chalkeios strongly oppose the continuation of the RIC in their area, citing issues such as overpopulation and unsanitary conditions, which pose challenges in their daily lives (31/12/20 P8). The appearance of makeshift shelters and occasional encroachments on private fields has prompted reactions from landowners, leading to firm opposition to the ongoing presence of the RIC in Vial and on the island of Chios. Although eventual compensation was extended to local residents for damages incurred by their fields, the process encountered prolonged delays, with some individuals remaining uncompensated as of the interview period (January/March 2021). Respondents attribute these delays to bureaucratic inefficiencies within the Ministry. Implicitly, these narratives suggest the violation of property rights among indigenous residents.

Under these circumstances, a significant concern arises from the dissemination of fake news by extremist factions, subsequently amplified by local media channels, leading to the unwarranted stigmatization of refugees. The Chios local community is exhibiting xenophobic reactions fueled by misinformation. Notably, in narratives, there is a direct acknowledgment of the human rights of refugees enshrined in international law, prominently exemplified by the right to education.

> A negative incident in Chios occurred when individuals attempted to collect signatures to prevent seven-year-old refugee children from attending school, citing concerns about diseases. Fortunately, this did not materialize and the children went to school without any issues.
>
> (14/01/21 P13)

From an alternative narrative, the island faces a distinct challenge in the realm of tourism. Examining tourism through a temporal lens reveals a discernible decline in tourism indicators over the past decade, predating the onset of refugee inflows. Various factors, including the repercussions of the 2009 economic crisis and the indigenous community's reservations toward tourism, are attributed to this downturn. Chios, in particular, failed to position itself competitively in charter flights, having neglected the development of its tourism sector in recent years. Contrary to conventional understanding, different local actors posit that the influx of refugees paradoxically engendered a form of unconventional 'tourism'. This phenomenon manifested through the prolonged presence of international organizations (IOs) and NGOs personnel, security forces officers and the refugees themselves, who assumed roles as consumers. Consequently, there ensued an upswing in tourist expenditures, underscored by heightened demand for services encompassing restaurants, taxis and supermarkets. Furthermore, this surge prompted an expansion in shipping routes, escalating from a thrice-weekly frequency to six times a week. Compounding this intricate scenario, staffing at the RIC predominantly drew from the local populace, or, alternatively, attracted individuals from abroad who relocated to the island to partake in activities intricately linked to the RIC. This intricate interplay between the refugee influx and its multifaceted impact on the island's economic dynamics, particularly within the tourism sector, underscores the complexity of the challenges faced by Chios (14/01/21 P12; 14/01/21 P13).

On the contrary, dissenting narratives among local actors challenge the purported benefits ('pros') attributed to the influx of refugees, particularly in terms of purportedly 'balancing the tourist offer' and contributing positively to the island's overall economy. In these counter-narratives, economic activities revolving around immigrants are construed with negative implications. Primarily, islands hosting RICs find themselves susceptible to economic downturn, given the substantial reliance on immigration as a cornerstone of their economic framework. The economic landscape undergoes a discernible deviation from what is considered a 'healthy economy', creating a cyclical pattern fueled by the management of immigration on the islands. This narrative underscores the transformative impact on the economic and social fabric of the island, emphasizing a shift toward a migrant economy that, in certain instances, operates within the realm of an undeclared economy. Instances include the noncompliance of rental premises with tax regulations and the lack of transparency in the procurement practices of NGOs.

The rotational dynamics of suppliers and NGOs involved in providing services to refugees emerge as a central concern. Within this narrative framework, profit generation from refugee flows by NGOs and suppliers is juxtaposed against the perilous circumstances faced by asylum seekers approaching the Aegean islands. The paradoxical observation is articulated that asylum seekers originating from Algeria and Morocco opt for entry through the eastern Mediterranean borders rather than choosing Spain as their European gateway. This narrative posits that such choices are not arbitrary but deliberate, guided by certain directives (25/02/21 P20). This particular perspective places paramount importance on sustaining the refugee population and augmenting the professional turnover of those engaged in this sector. NGOs, in this context, are met with skepticism. The directional trajectory of migration toward the islands is reframed not as a spontaneous, haphazard movement, but as a phenomenon potentially subject to guidance. While the narrative acknowledges the imperative of safeguarding the right to life for asylum seekers, the primary focus pivots toward advocating policy alterations concerning the submission of asylum claims in the context of migration flows to the islands. The chief concern, apart from the safeguarding of asylum seekers' lives, revolves around protecting the interests of the local community grappling with the ramifications of refugee flows on their island.

Simultaneously, the recruitment of security forces officers or border guards is portrayed as not conducive to the developmental interests of the islands. It is asserted that the five islands collectively bear 'the brunt of the immigration', as RICs, initially conceived as reception and identification centers, have evolved into protracted-stay facilities due to the 'geographical restriction' mandating asylum seekers to remain on the islands for extended periods. Consequently, this narrative highlights instances where, during periods when the refugee population reached 7,500–8,000 on Chios, housing a population of 50,000, the ratio of the 'native population' to the 'immigrant population' hovered between 15% and 16%. Another factor that reduces the proportion of the native population is the people involved in migration management (e.g., legal advisers of asylum seekers, employees of various IOs, NGOs, catering). Moreover, the integration of the migrant population into society is characterized as occurring 'abruptly' (25/02/21 P20).

Moreover, predominant among the highlighted social challenges are issues stemming from the exodus of the younger demographic from the islands, a consequence attributed to a lack of vocational rehabilitation. Concurrently, the island's populace is grappling with an aging demographic juxtaposed against a concurrent surge in both the migrant population and individuals affiliated with the burgeoning migrant economy. Within the regional context of the North Aegean, to which Chios pertains, a noteworthy designation as one of Greece's and Europe's most economically deprived regions is conferred. This narrative contends that the Gross Domestic Product witnessed a precipitous decline post-2015–2016, coinciding with the upswing in migration influx to the islands. A third facet of the narrative underscores the social quandaries posed by cultural disparities among refugees. Within such a sizable population, disparities in cultural norms emerge, with individuals diverging significantly from the European way of life, thereby introducing potential challenges stemming from inadvertent clashes of differing values and customs. The narrative deliberately draws attention to the dichotomy between the established community, denoted as the 'native population' and the 'others', namely, the migrant populace (25/02/21 P20). This narrative aligns itself within the sphere of 'partiality', as elucidated in the preceding chapter, specifically falling under the category of communitarianism. Noteworthy is the absence of explicit reference to human rights within this narrative, with a pronounced focus on concepts such as 'community', 'society' and 'cultural differences'. The narrative underscores a palpable demarcation between the 'native population' and the categorization of 'others'.

EU–Turkey statement: its impact on the RIC of Chios

The EU–Turkey Statement[1] has been appraised as a legal instrument yielding consequential outcomes for all Aegean islands hosting RICs. The salient repercussions of this accord are discernible primarily in the following dimensions: (a) the substantial overreach of asylum seeker numbers surpassing the operational capacities of the RIC, (b) the protracted duration of asylum seekers' stay, (c) the subjection of asylum seekers to ostensibly inhumane conditions, encompassing habitation in weather-exposed tents, challenges in accessing health services, protracted waits for the processing of asylum procedures and an overarching sense of insecurity regarding the future (02/04/21 P26; 25/02/21 P20; 14/01/21 P12; 14/01/21 P13) and (d) a perceptible shift in the resident population's attitudes toward asylum seekers, manifesting as an escalating trend of racism on the islands (03/12/20 P8).

According to insights provided by local actors, during the initial phase of refugee flows to Chios, a considerable segment of the local community demonstrated solidarity with the arriving refugees. Notably, from the end of July 2015 until the beginning of November 2015, the central garden adjacent to the island's town, which served as the sole verdant space, accommodated asylum seekers for a brief duration before they proceeded to other destinations. However, the transformation in societal sentiment did not transpire in January/February 2016, coinciding with the initiation of the RIC, but rather evolved gradually subsequent to the enforcement of the EU–Turkey Statement.

This agreement compelled asylum seekers to endure prolonged stays on the island, in stark contrast to the preagreement period when their time in the camp was restricted to a duration ranging from three days to one week (02/04/21 P26; 25/02/21 P20; 14/01/21 P12; 14/01/21 P13). The primary quandary engendered by the EU–Turkey Deal manifests in the creation of conditions tantamount to entrapment and restriction on the islands. Grounded in the specific 'joint statement', the Greek government has instituted the so-called 'geographic restriction'. Within this framework, an intricate situation of 'artificial stay' and 'artificial confinement' unfolds. Despite a complete absence of migratory flows to the islands during the period of the interviews (February 2021), the RIC persisted in a state of overcrowding. This correlation implies that the overpopulation in the existing RIC serves as a mechanism to influence local communities, persuading them of the imperative for a novel asylum seekers' camp (02/04/21 P26; 25/02/21 P20; 14/01/21 P12; 14/01/21 P13). Consequently, local consent becomes pivotal for the creation of a larger structure. In this narrative the principles of positive law are imposed, implicitly distinguishing between positive law and soft law, as evidenced in the characterization of the EU–Turkey Deal as a 'joint statement'. The narrative further delves into the legal remedies employed, including appeals and the eventual vindication sought through the verdict of the Council of State (CoE/ΣτΕ). Such measures were orchestrated to contest the constitutionality of the 'geographical restriction' imposed on the Aegean islands. Notably, the narrative indirectly references the 'right to movement' of asylum seekers, asserting the geographical restriction as unconstitutional in alignment with the pertinent decision of the Hellenic Council of State (CoE/ΣτΕ) (25/02/21 P20).

According to local actors in Chios, a discernible polarization exists in the aftermath of this agreement, categorizing a limited minority as anti-racists and attributing a substantial portion with holding racist views. This narrative accentuates the adverse consequences of EU public policy on societal unity and prevailing solidarity toward refugees (14/01/21 P12; 14/01/21 P13). Implicitly, this perspective underscores the importance of safeguarding refugee rights and posits a moral obligation on the local society. The latent impact of the accord surfaces as it exacerbates the crisis of solidarity, stemming from the inadvertent entrenchment of asylum seekers on the islands. Within this milieu, the accord distinctly shapes the dynamics of refugee solidarity. Situated within the framework of the glocalization of human rights, there is a palpable diminution in the potential for the realization of human rights.

Conflicts of interest in Chios: a clash of human rights and EU policies?

In Chios, local actors identify a conflict between human rights for asylum seekers and EU political determinations. They highlight human rights violations and harsh living conditions in the RIC. The narrative underscores asylum seekers' perilous journeys due to threats like war or political persecution. Conversely, the EU is seen as ostensibly humanitarian but imposes challenging conditions at entry points to deter refugee flows. These decisions compound challenges in the RIC, limiting agency for local entities (08/03/21 P21). In these restrictive contexts, local representatives, encompassing municipal councilors, the mayor, the regional council and the regional governor are urged to navigate a dual trajectory within the framework of glocalized human rights. On one front, their imperative is to champion the protection of asylum seekers' rights by ameliorating living conditions. Simultaneously, they must address and mitigate adverse repercussions on the local community.

Conversely, actors highlight that tensions arise within local communities when a municipality serves as a 'persuasive instrument' for a 'phobic and extreme right-wing policy', amplifying such ideologies through its rhetoric and actions within the local sphere. In the complex interplay between the human rights of refugees and EU policies that instrumentalize refugees to deter migration flows, local and regional governments may possess comparatively circumscribed latitude for intervention. Nonetheless, they possess the capacity to advocate for the human rights of asylum seekers, localizing human rights and thereby mitigating the emergence of extreme nationalist and fascist phenomena.

In concordance with prevailing narratives, it is underscored that both the Greek government and the European Union exhibit a notable deficiency in credibility. In the Chios context, the diminished credibility of the Greek government becomes conspicuous through its failure to honor the agreement for the cessation of the 'three years use' of the privately owned space within the municipality, housing the RIC. Specifically, the RIC, slated to cease operations in the designated area in Vial by December 2018, continued unabated despite the accreditation granted in 2015 by the then-minister to the then-mayor. The overarching sentiment among actors adheres to the perspective that 'refugees are not an enemy of the local society'; rather, they are victims. Concurrently, the society of Chios is portrayed as a victim as long as the RIC remains situated in this locale (14/01/21 P12). This narrative explicitly delineates reference to the rights of refugees and identifies the policies of the European Union as the primary locus of conflicts between refugee rights and EU policies. The management of the RIC by successive Greek governments has led to a schism among the citizens of the island, dichotomizing them into 'solidarists' and the 'rest'. Solidarists are met with suspicion, subject to attacks and perceived as adversaries seeking to establish RICs on the islands. Post-2016, incidents of racism and xenophobia have become more pronounced. The island's mayor has faced accusations of racist comments and has exhibited a nonamicable stance toward asylum seekers (03/12/21 P8).

Metaphors in the narratives about the RIC at Chios

The RIC in Vial has been starkly characterized by local actors as resembling a 'concentration camp', where asylum seekers endure long queues for basic necessities such as water, food, medical attention and contact with asylum services. Reports from NGOs highlight instances of abuse and exploitation within the center. The prevailing narrative among local actors paints the concept of the RIC as 'punitive' and 'inhumane'. Efforts to address these issues have included proposals for collaborative management between the municipality and the ministry, aiming to mitigate the camp-like conditions. Some councilors advocated for the active involvement of asylum seekers in the daily operations of the RIC, suggesting tasks such as cleaning and cooking as a means for them to contribute positively to the center's community. However, these proposals were largely overlooked by the Ministry. Amidst these challenges, reports of human rights violations persist, documenting 'deplorable and inhumane living conditions' and 'punitive treatment' against refugees.

> When Mr. Verwey, who was responsible for implementing the EU-Turkey Deal, visited our island and held a closed meeting to persuade us to accept a closed center, we emphasized the need to improve conditions at the Reception and Identification Center (RIC). However, he made it clear that there was no intention to improve conditions because the message to be conveyed abroad was that living conditions on the island were not favorable. Therefore, the inhumane conditions at the RIC were not attributed to incompetence or lack of resources but were a deliberate choice. Consequently, these camps are inherently 'punitive concentration' camps.
>
> (14/01/21 P12)

Municipal councilors propose alternative options and solutions to prevent the establishment of Closed Controlled Structures, such as accommodating asylum seekers in hotels and houses. However, narratives emphasize that the existence of RICs is a political decision of the European Union, aiming to create 'island fortresses' and 'island prisons,' while the Greek government complies with these directives. Asylum seekers on the island are trapped in an intractable state of limbo, awaiting resolution and uncertain about their future.

Fake news is exacerbating problems within the local community, often serving the interests of certain elected local government officials who present themselves as 'refugee fighters', purportedly committed to combatting the presence of refugees (14/01/21 P13). Local actors note that Chios confronts distinct challenges owing to its close geographical proximity to Turkey and its designation as a border region (14/01/21 P13), which has contributed to the development of a strong sense of nationalism within the local community. However, according to municipal councilors, following the establishment of the RIC on the island, a segment of the local community underwent a shift, associating 'nationalist' sentiments with 'racist' tendencies for the first time, turning against refugees. This transformation was attributed, firstly, to the implications of the EU–Turkey Statement and secondly, to Erdogan's actions (14/01/21 P12). Specifically, in March 2020 in Evros, Erdogan manipulated refugees to advance his own agenda (14/01/21 P12; 25/02/21 P20). Within this narrative, the portrayal emerged that 'illegal immigrants arrive on the islands as invaders' with the intention of 'changing our culture,' facilitating Erdogan's purported 'Islamization of the islands' (14/01/21 P12). Post the EU–Turkey Agreement and the ensuing shift within the local community, asylum seekers were branded as 'invaders.' Conversely, on Chios, asylum seekers are ironically labeled 'investors' to juxtapose them with the 'wealthy tourists' ideally expected on the island. This term, 'investors', is employed to deflect from any accusations of racist discourse (03/12/20 P8).

The EU–Turkey Statement of 2016 is characterized as a 'key point' both for the asylum seekers themselves and for its impact on public opinion, which shifted local society against refugees due to its prolongation of asylum seekers' stay on the islands. The agreement utilized the concept of the 'sea as a border' to effectively confine these individuals to the islands and address Europe's refugee crisis. This containment strategy was crucial, as it prevented asylum seekers from relocating to Attica, a gateway to other Western European countries, thereby mitigating the continent's migrant inflow (14/01/21 P12). According to this narrative, the agreement imposed what can be termed 'double borders' upon the local population of Chios, entailing a border with Turkey on one side and one with Greece on the other.

> In some cases, when you leave by car, they open the car boot to check if you are hiding someone (an asylum seeker).
>
> (14/01/21 P12)

Consequently, a segment of society underwent a transformation, marked by the resurgence of nationalism and racism. In concert with the political decisions of both the EU and Greek administrations, the three islands were effectively bestowed upon Golden Dawn, the extremist right-wing party. In essence, Golden Dawn inherited the support of the islands' voters as a 'gift'. The pervasive influence of racist narratives has significantly shaped the local populace, a reality evident in the outcomes of recent local government elections, as highlighted by certain observers. Specifically, six councilors affiliated with a particular faction have secured seats on the municipal council, some of whom have historical ties to the 'Panchiaki Epitropi Agona'. A local actor asserts that these municipal councilors harbor latent racist sentiments.

> When you examine their texts, you'll notice they're meticulously crafted, often authored by educated professionals like lawyers and engineers who

> are esteemed members of Chios society. However, despite their outward appearance, they harbor blatant racist views. This is evident in the fact that six municipal councilors, who likely secured around 15% of the vote in the municipal elections, are aligned with them. Moreover, they garnered 1,300 signatures to impede child asylum-seekers from attending school—a significant figure for Chios. Thus, we're witnessing a society that, driven by certain political decisions, has veered toward the extreme right. However, it's important to note that not everyone in this spectrum can be labeled as fascists.
>
> (14/01/21 P12)

According to the same narrative, the signing of the EU–Turkey Statement resulted in the islands being likened to prisons. This agreement is hence characterized as a turning point, as the conditions it created contributed to the escalation of racism and fascism. As noted by local actors, Chios in 2014 was among the prefectures with the lowest rates of support for Golden Dawn.

Residents and councilors from various factions are opposed to the RIC in Vial and simultaneously resist the establishment of a new Closed Controlled Structure in Chios. According to local sources, following the ordeal with Vial, there is widespread aversion to having a RIC 'in their backyard'. The RIC, as described by municipal councilors, is akin to a 'shanty town' hosting 3,000 asylum seekers (previously numbering 5,000–6,000), situated adjacent to the modest village of Chalkeios, which itself comprises only 500 inhabitants. Local narratives highlight how the Vial RIC has been portrayed in the media as posing risks to public health, affecting both the refugees and the local population. Another perspective underscores the metamorphosis of Chios into an immigration-dependent economy, despite the local community's resistance; residents advocate for 'sustainable development'. According to this narrative, the concentration of asylum seekers in the RIC perpetuates Chios's identity as either a 'prison island' or a 'refugee island' (25/02/21 P20).

Note

1 Some of the local actors interviewed do not accept the term 'agreement' as the EU–Turkey Statement is translated in Greek; from local actors, it is conceived as a 'text' that is a 'joint statement'.

6 Cos, Pyli

Municipality of Cos has a permanent population of 19,432 inhabitants (Hellenic Statistical Authority, census 2011) and the total population of the island is 33,388 people (Hellenic Statistical Authority, census 2011). The municipality of Cos includes, among others, the municipal community of Dikaiou to which belongs the Municipal Community of Asfendi and the Municipal Community of Pyli. The Municipal Community of Pyli includes Marmari and Pyli. The Reception and Identification Center (RIC) at Cos is located in Pyli. The official capacity of the RIC on the island was 816 people, but in 2019 the structure accommodated 4,119 asylum seekers, while in 2020 the number of those residing in the structure decreased to 863 asylum seekers (Ministry of Immigration and Asylum, annual report 12/2020). During the period of the interviews, the mayor of the municipality of Cos was Theodosios Nikitaras with the faction 'Strong Cos' and the municipal council consisted of the municipal factions 'Dynami Allagis', 'Orama kai Drasi' and 'Laiki Syspeirosi Cos' (communist party).

Empirical research on the RIC of Pyli, Cos

Pre-2015, the island of Cos experienced intermittent instances of asylum seeker arrivals, typically comprising a modest cohort of five to ten individuals over extended intervals – a magnitude perceived as tolerable by the local community. However, the onset of the migration crisis in the summer of 2015 precipitated a substantial escalation in asylum seeker arrivals to Cos town, leading to a notable surge in numbers (22/12/20 P10; 22/01/21 P15; 08/05/21 P27), eventually reaching an estimated count of 13,000 individuals.

> The migration surged suddenly in the summer of 2015, resulting in approximately 13,000 people congregating in Cos, dispersed throughout the town, including its historical commercial and administrative center. However, there was no clear policy from either the European Union or our country. This marked the first occurrence of such a situation, catching everyone unprepared and leading to tragic circumstances.
>
> (18/02/21 P18)

DOI: 10.4324/9781003468134-10

The site chosen for the RIC in Pyli, Cos, originally comprised an abandoned camp. In 2015, coinciding with heightened immigration flows to the island, discussions ensued regarding the selection of a suitable location. These deliberations occurred between the contemporaneous government and the municipal authority, which held responsibilities until September 2019. However, the management at the local level unfolded within a discordant framework, characterized by a lack of alternative proposals and substantive realism. Consequently, the municipality's perspective was marginalized, as decisions were made without due consideration, reflecting a disregard for its input in establishing the facility at the specified location. According to the current municipal administration, this oversight was avoidable and the establishment of the RIC could have occurred in an alternative location strategically positioned 'distant from any settlement' to mitigate visibility.

The demographic composition of the RIC in Pyli underwent a marked escalation, surging to an approximate count of 4,500 asylum seekers in 2019, a notable departure from its original design to accommodate 900 individuals. The municipal responsibilities of Cos primarily extend to waste collection outside the RIC premises, presenting a challenge as this service, typically associated with fee collection, is not undertaken by the municipality (22/12/20 P10; 22/01/21 P15; 18/02/21 P18; 08/05/21 P27). Despite the municipality's acknowledgment of primary jurisdiction resting with the military and police, they affirm their commitment to providing assistance in a spirit of goodwill and collaboration. Within this operational framework, the municipal authority extends its support to the RIC with the overarching objective of safeguarding the well-being of Cos residents, fostering local economic stability and nurturing societal cohesion, as illuminated in local discourse (18/02/21 P18). In this context, the glocalization of human rights concerns primarily revolves around the islanders, as municipal authorities prioritize the protection of the Indigenous community and the vested interests and human rights of its members. Notably, the narrative places lesser emphasis on the rights of asylum seekers, thus relegating their prominence within this discourse.

Challenges in the RIC of Cos

A pivotal challenge underscored in the principal discourse surrounding the RIC in Pyli pertains to its ethnic and religious dynamics, encompassing a mosaic of 48 distinct nationalities and diverse religious affiliations. This complexity extends further to encompass socioeconomic heterogeneity and the presence of unaccompanied children. Despite the inherent tensions arising from this intricate mix, the prevailing characterization in the narrative deems the situation as generally 'manageable'. Most notably, the asylum seekers exhibit comprehension and cooperation. The unique dynamics encountered at the RIC in Cos differentiate it from analogous centers on other islands, as delineated in the narrative dated (18/02/21 P18). Within this narrative, the management of the RIC is characterized by inherent elements of uncertainty and risk. Beyond the confines of administrative responsibilities, latent issues surface, occasionally intertwined with broader realms such as 'national politics' and 'artificial tension'. These dimensions introduce an additional layer of complexity, contributing to the nuanced and intricate management landscape of the RIC in Pyli. This narrative particularly underscores the coexistence of diverse groups within the RIC and the potential conflicts that may ensue among them. Notably absent from this narrative is a pronounced emphasis on asylum seekers´ human rights; instead, the focus centers on the collective will of the involved actors, fostering cooperative interactions among the resident communities (18/02/21 P18).

An alternate narrative scrutinizes the asylum procedures within the context of contending with the pandemic, as elucidated in various sources (22/12/20 P10; 22/01/21 P15; 18/02/21 P18; 08/05/21 P27). Commencing from April 2020, following the assumption of command by the RIC administrator, a cohort of 2,500 asylum seekers found residence in the Cos RIC, coinciding with the onset of the coronavirus pandemic. The primary objective during this period was the safeguarding of the health of both asylum seekers and staff members. This narrative underscores the uninterrupted continuity of asylum application procedures throughout the pandemic, culminating in the successful prevention of any positive COVID-19 cases within the RIC premises (08/05/21 P27). This narrative is characterized by its depiction of the harmonious cohabitation of asylum seekers within the RIC, emphasizing successful measures taken to mitigate emergent challenges. Notably absent is any explicit or implicit reference to human rights; the narrative predominantly centers on the administrative apparatus's adaptability to absorb and navigate unforeseen disruptions.

Another narrative identifies as a positive development that occurred in January 2020, a revision of the legislative framework. The revised procedures are characterized as both 'stricter and shorter', aiming to reduce the time intervals between asylum examinations and limit the duration for potential objections from asylum seekers concerned (18/02/21 P18). Within this perspective, the local actor's narrative emphasizes the pivotal role of the legislative framework governing asylum procedures. The stringent nature of the asylum legislative framework is viewed positively, emphasizing the necessity for intensified and expedited procedures. Notably, this narrative does not explicitly consider the rights of asylum seekers. The focal point remains the local community of Cos, with the primary objective of alleviating the congestion of the RIC on the island through the acceleration of asylum application reviews.

In an alternative narrative, the expedited examination of asylum applications and procedures may be associated with potential infringements on human rights, while multifaceted challenges at distinct levels are underscored. First, the expedited processing of asylum procedures raises consequential concerns that may implicate human rights violations. Specifically, outlined challenges encompass: (a) the precarious conditions stemming from the hastened pace of asylum procedures, which, in certain instances, may result in inadequately scrutinized asylum examinations and (b) precarious conditions arising from the repatriation of individuals to their countries as a means of expediently 'disposing of' asylum applications (22/12/20 P10). This narrative is prominently centered on the rights of asylum seekers, manifesting explicit apprehension about potential transgressions of the right to nonrefoulement for asylum seekers (as articulated in the principle and Article 33 of the 1951 Geneva Convention on Refugees and its 1967 Protocol) before the comprehensive examination of their asylum claims. Moreover, the suspension of the ESTIA housing program for vulnerable asylum seekers led to uncertainties regarding the resettlement or reintegration of certain asylum seeker groups and impediments in the domain of education, particularly the absence of children attending formal public educational structures. Notably, in 2018, children engaged with Refugee Support and Education Structures (ΔΥΕΠ), but faced delays in registrations, commencing typically around January, midway through the academic year. Consequently, children resort to informal education provided by organizations like ARSIS - Association for the Social Support of Youth through the KEDU program in Cos, with KEDU aspiring to integrate children into formal education structures (22/12/20 P10). This narrative distinctly accentuates the rights of asylum seekers. This narrative explicitly brings to the forefront the fundamental right to seek asylum, emphasizing the imperative of genuine access to the asylum procedure through equitable scrutiny of individual requests. Moreover, it expressly acknowledges the vulnerable status of children and highlights the indispensable right to education for refugee children. This narrative places a discernible emphasis on the centrality of human rights, specifically pertaining to the asylum process and the educational rights (No. 2 prot. No. 1 European Convention on Human Rights [ECHR]) of vulnerable groups, such as children within the refugee context.

Within a narrative, attention is drawn to the absence of medical care facilities within the RIC of Cos, coupled with a shortage of health personnel, thereby asserting that the prevailing conditions within the RIC degrade the dignity of its inhabitants (22/12/20 P10; 22/01/21 P15). Implicit in this discourse is an allusion to the right to health, as well as a tacit invocation of the violation of Article 3 of the ECHR concerning inhuman and degrading treatment. This violation is intricately tied to positive obligations to furnish complimentary medical care (a linkage expounded upon by Kolliniati 2019 regarding Article 3 of the ECHR and the provision of free healthcare). It is narrated that the exigencies prevailing within the Refugee and Migrant RIC transcend the confines of the facility, precipitating a direct and profound impact on the broader community of Cos. Accordingly, a nuanced comprehension of the challenges inherent to the RIC mandates a comprehensive acknowledgment of the interwoven challenges concurrently experienced by the local community of Cos (22/01/21 P15).

Challenges in Cos due to the existence of the RIC at Pyli

The intricacies of the local economy and the adept management of tensions to safeguard the well-being of the Indigenous community on the island are underlined in a narrative. This approach is facilitated through the municipal administration, which strives to forestall tensions and alleviate discontent among the local populace. It is noteworthy that concerted efforts are directed toward averting disillusionment among the residents identified as ‘ours’ or ‘the people of Cos’. According to this narrative, the local actors are conceived as pivotal players, underlying that distinct regions and municipalities possess the capacity to navigate the presence of the RICs in diverse manners (18/02/21 P18).

It is narrated that the intrusion of substantial migration flows disrupted the tranquility of Cos, a traditionally tourist-oriented island, where the local community grapples with the novelty of diversity. Stable and persistent programs and organizations are deemed instrumental in fostering positive cooperation initiatives, affording the community time to acclimate to the unfamiliar (22/12/20 P10). Conversely, a local actor contends that the presence of the RIC exacerbated xenophobic and racist sentiments on the island, directing hostilities toward the victims (refugees) rather than the architects of the RIC (22/01/21 P15). Simultaneously, issues arising in the village of Pyli attributed to the RIC's presence intertwine with the facility's daily operational challenges, including the absence of a drainage system. The hasty establishment of the structure is highlighted, with the narrative suggesting deliberate inaction by both local and national authorities to promptly address this specific predicament (22/01/21 P15).

An alternative perspective highlights tourism as a predominant challenge for Cos, framing it as the primary economic activity on the island. Preceding the pandemic, Cos, a renowned tourist destination, ranking as the third most visited destination in Greece and the foremost relative to its population and geographical expanse. The influx of migrants during the 2015–2016 period coincided with a decline in tourist arrivals, indicating the susceptibility of the tourism sector to external factors (18/02/21 P18; 08/05/21 P27). The RIC is viewed unfavorably at an economic level, impacting local tourism by prompting negotiations for reduced prices among tour operators, hoteliers and apartment owners due to social uncertainty on the island. This narrative underscores the heightened economic vulnerability of Cos, especially in the face of uncontrolled shifts in immigration patterns. Unlike other islands like Lesvos, where economic stakes are less pronounced, Cos heavily relies on tourism, constituting over 90% of its economic activity and fostering a monoculture of tourism. The narrative emphasizes that one of Cos's competitive advantages is its status as a secure tourist destination (18/02/21 P18).

It is asserted that the local community actively seeks to disassociate the immigrant presence from the island's economic landscape. A prevailing sentiment among the local community advocates for the inland relocation of asylum seekers (08/05/21 P27). In an alternate narrative, the RIC primarily impacted the workforce, not major hotel proprietors, leveraging low occupancy rates to dissuade workers from seeking improved conditions and enhanced remuneration (22/01/21 P15).

Moreover, certain local narratives underscore foreign policy considerations, emphasizing the geopolitical significance of the island's strategic location in the Aegean. Specifically, a narrative pertaining to the North and South-East Aegean islands interlinks the Greek state's sovereignty with their specific geographical positions. This narrative posits the crucial geopolitical role of these islands in foreign policy, given their proximity to Turkey. Consequently, the municipal authority of Cos opposes the establishment of a new Closed Controlled Structure on the island. Urgently removing the islands from the 'migration map' is advocated, aligning with Greece's sovereignty concerns (18/02/21 P18). This narrative refrains from explicit references to human rights but focalizes on the notion of sovereignty, advocating for the relocation of the RIC from the islands to safeguard national sovereignty. The emphasis lies in the geopolitical positioning of the island, strategically intertwined with the broader concept of the country's sovereignty.

EU–Turkey statement: its impact on the RIC of Cos

The EU–Turkey Agreement is portrayed in a narrative as a commendable framework, acknowledged for its efficacy in curtailing migration flows during the 2017–2018 period in comparison to the influx experienced in 2015–2016. Characterized as an 'initial success', the agreement is credited with yielding positive outcomes and facilitating some returns to Turkey. However, its implementation on the part of Turkey lapsed, ostensibly due to the onset of the COVID-19 pandemic and as of the interview period extending until May 2021, its nonimplementation persisted. Despite this hiatus, proponents of the agreement argue that its positive track record justifies the imperative for its reinstatement and continued dialogue with Turkey. Sustaining the collaborative efforts remains crucial for effecting the repatriation of individuals deemed ineligible for asylum following negative decisions at both levels of the asylum examination process and who lack entitlement to prolonged residence in Greece (05/08/21 P27).

Conversely, an alternative narrative scrutinizing the EU–Turkey Agreement identifies several inherent challenges. The agreement designates Turkey as a 'safe country' for the repatriation of asylum seekers. However, this perspective contends that the blanket characterization of Turkey as inherently secure does not hold true for various demographic groups. Specifically, it is argued that Turkey is not deemed safe for the Syrian Kurds, highlighting a nuanced and population-specific dimension to the notion of safety (22/12/20 P10). In another account the impact of the EU–Turkey Agreement on the influx of arrivals is scrutinized, positing that the Turkish President strategically leverages the agreement to advance personal objectives. Observable fluctuations in migration patterns to the islands coincide with periods of nonimplementation of the EU–Turkey Agreement, often aligning with heightened tensions in the European Union's dealings with Turkey or Greece. Furthermore, statements made by the Turkish President have been identified as catalysts for increased migration flows during these periods. Concurrently, individuals from the opposing Turkish coast are noted to migrate to the islands during such phases, with official support from the Turkish state amplifying this movement (18/02/21 P18).

Conflicts of interests in Cos: balancing financial interests

Within the discourses of local actors, the contention arises that the dynamics on the island lack a conflict of interests but rather manifest a state of equilibrium. The reduction in tourism stemming from migration and earthquake events found equilibrium through an augmented demand for accommodations for workers employed in the structures or affiliated services. Notably, certain small-scale hotel establishments, intermittently operational, allocated their premises to individuals whose residence expenses were covered by entities like the United Nations High Commissioner for Refugees. Simultaneously, the influx of additional workers associated with the RIC, either internally or externally, led them to seek housing within the local market. This narrative interprets the resultant economic shift not as a conflict of interests but as a harmonious balance. It contends that the demand was met by the supply from apartments and modest establishments, which, lacking competitiveness within the tourist circuit due to their age, opportunistically availed themselves of the chance to lease their establishments for a period. In this conceptualization, the economic transition adhered to the principles of the law of supply and demand, suggesting a seamless evolution from one state to the other.

> For instance, there are individuals currently residing on our island as part of the security forces, solely employed by the RIC; otherwise, there would be no reason for them to be here.
>
> (18/02/21 P18)

In a similar discourse, it is asserted that the absence of statistical evidence renders untenable any direct correlation between a decline in tourism and the presence of the RIC structure. The economic data available fails to substantiate claims that the structure has had an adverse impact on the island's economic vitality. Conversely, the establishment of the RIC led to the generation of new employment opportunities, exemplified by the recruitment of border guards and an expanded market for rental residences. Notwithstanding the divergent perspectives and interpretations concerning the structural effects on the island's economy, certain local actors perceive an absence of conflict of interest in this regard (08/05/21 P27). It is asserted that, despite a segment of the local community deriving financial benefits from the presence of the RIC, there is a conspicuous absence of public endorsement for the RIC's existence. This strategic avoidance of public advocacy aligns with the prevailing sentiment within the local society, where the majority expresses opposition to the continued presence of the RIC structure (22/12/20 P10).

Metaphors in the narratives about the RIC at Cos

One narrative delineates Cos and other islands hosting RICs as the vanguard of Greece's national sovereignty in the eastern Aegean. Consequently, there is an urgent call for Cos to swiftly exit the 'migration map' to cease being the vulnerable 'soft underbelly' during periods of uncertainty, political tension or expansionist territorial ambitions (18/02/21 P18). Migration flows are metaphorically characterized as a 'game' by a local actor, prompting the implementation of policies designed to curb flows. These policies involve heightened aerial surveillance and fortified maritime borders through increased resources and personnel for the port authority, resulting in a tangible reduction in migration flows. The specific measures enhance the probability of apprehensions and returns, serving as a deterrent for both traffickers and asylum seekers. In this narrative, these policies 'count' and give a positive sign for the effort being made to reduce flows or at least send the message 'to the neighboring shore' that they are controlling 'the flow game'. Nevertheless, according to this interpretation, the pivotal factor influencing immigration dynamics lies in 'the relationship with the neighboring country' and the broader EU–Turkey relationship. Greece is portrayed as 'vulnerable' and a 'weak link', with each instance of disturbance to the EU–Turkey Agreement translating into increased migration flows impacting Greece (18/02/21 P18).

In an alternative narrative, instances of obscenity are highlighted. For instance, as refugee flows commenced, certain establishments requested money from refugees to charge their mobile phones. In other examples, employers, in collaboration with the RIC, were legally permitted to hire refugees and asylum seekers from specific nationalities, thereby exploiting an inexpensive labor force residing within the RIC. In local actor's narrative is mentioned that «Last February, a Palestinian refugee demanded the debts from his employer, while the employer threatened him and ran over him with his car, causing serious health problems for the Palestinian refugee» (22/01/21 P15). This narrative explicitly addresses the infringement of labor rights, the presence of exploitative working conditions and instances of undisclosed employment. Additionally, some nongovernmental organizations operating in the refugee domain were reported to secure multimillion grants, allegedly 'stepping on the need' of asylum seekers to 'generate profits unashamedly'.

7 Leros, Lepida

The municipality of Leros has a permanent population of 7,917 inhabitants (Hellenic Statistical Authority, census 2011). During the interview period (2020–2021) in Leros, there was a RIC (Registration and Identification Center) in Lepida and a temporary Hospitality Structure in PIKPA which stopped operating in 2020 by decision of the Minister of Immigration and Asylum. Our research focused on the RIC in Lepida. The official capacity of the RIC was 860 people, but in 2019 the structure accommodated 2,757 asylum seekers, while in 2020 only 667 asylum seekers resided in the structure (Ministry of Immigration and Asylum, annual report 12/2020). The mayor of the municipality of Leros at the time of the interviews was, for the third consecutive term, Michael Kollias with the municipal political party 'Leros, me orama kai schedio gia olous'. In different narratives of local actors, it is mentioned that Leros is 'acquainted with the different', as since the end of the fifties a psychiatric hospital was created and operated on the island, while in the end of the sixties political exiles were sent to the island.

Empirical research on the RIC of Lepida, Leros

The primary RIC on Leros, established in March 2016, occupied an expansive field surrounding a facility for individuals with mental illnesses, utilizing prefabricated structures. Recognizing Leros as a pivotal entry point, the municipality sought the creation of the RIC. During interviews, local actors consistently characterized Leros as the 'paradise of RICs' in comparison to others in the Aegean region. The prevailing narrative on the island asserts that Leros represents a unique case with a history intricately linked to the community's adept handling of diversity (01/12/20 P6; 01/12/20 P7; 21/12/20 P9; 22/01/21 P16; 23/02/21 P19; 09/03/21 P22; 09/05/21 P28). Factors such as the island's historical background, the community's interactions with various groups and the manageable scale of asylum seekers distinguish the Lepida RIC, positioning it as a 'role model'. Leros, historically chosen to host groups like political prisoners and the mentally ill, is perceived as an exemplar, not due to any perceived shortcomings, but rather because of its existing facilities and historical context (23/02/21 P19). Although the establishment of the RIC partially addressed the initial needs, it concurrently inflicted considerable damage.

DOI: 10.4324/9781003468134-11

Despite encountering substantial challenges during the initial operational phase, subsequent improvements have been made to the conditions within the Leros RIC over time.

Challenges in the RIC of Leros

The prevailing narrative at Leros accentuates challenges akin to those encountered by other RICs scrutinized in this research. In the initial operational phase, the facility grappled with adverse conditions, necessitating the military's provision of sustenance to asylum seekers. Sanitary conditions were suboptimal, exacerbated by overcrowding, compelling many to inhabit alternative structures outside the RIC in deplorable conditions. Predominantly, a significant impediment resides in the protracted asylum procedures, contributing to overcrowding and prolonged stays within the RIC (01/12/20 P6; 01/12/20 P7; 21/12/20 P9; 22/01/21 P16; 23/02/21 P19; 09/03/21 P22; 09/05/21 P28), while the narrative surrounding the RIC on Leros underscores the presence of domestic violence and drug trafficking within its confines (01/12/20 P6).

Narratives elucidate instances where asylum seekers endured stays in the RIC spanning one to two years between 2018 and 2020, awaiting official decisions and necessary documentation (09/05/21 P28). Concurrently, interviews conducted at a later juncture reveal a reduction in the time required to grant asylum, with the waiting period fluctuating between six months to one year (23/02/21 P19). Pertinently, the absence of legal representation within the RIC exacerbates the plight of asylum seekers, who lack access to legal support. Medical care within the RIC is notably restricted, prompting prompt intervention from the Leros hospital to address emergent crises.

An additional formidable challenge pertains to the imperative provision of education for children residing in the RIC. The overarching objective is to facilitate the integration of children into formal educational frameworks, necessitating collaborative efforts from diverse agencies to implement supportive measures (21/12/20 P9). This narrative explicitly emphasizes the inherent right of refugee children to education.

Challenges in Leros due to the existence of the RIC at Lepida

In the narratives of local actors, it becomes apparent that the localization of human rights does not occur for either the asylum seekers or the inhabitants. As highlighted in the narrative, the proportion of asylum seekers to the local population was disproportionate on the island, with a period where 4,000 to 5,000 asylum seekers resided in the RIC, among the 8,000 inhabitants (23/02/21 P19; 09/05/21 P28; 09/03/21 P22). The architectural layout and personnel allocations were initially designed to meet the needs of the local population of Leros. However, these arrangements proved insufficient when faced with the significant influx of asylum seekers. According to the narrative, a recurring issue emerged where asylum seekers frequently sought medical attention at the hospital, sometimes without compelling necessity. It's noted as a challenge that these asylum seekers come from different cultures and often express a desire not to remain on the island.

Local actors in Leros emphasize the limited role of the municipal level, as decisions made by the democratically elected municipal council are disregarded by the central Greek government. Despite the direct impact of the RIC on Leros and its residents, the perspective of the local government is often overlooked. This oversight leads to a significant gap in meeting obligations related to protecting the human rights of asylum seekers within the RIC. The narrative acknowledges potential violations of the right to movement and freedom for those awaiting return to Turkey. Despite municipal efforts to address these issues and protect the rights of asylum seekers, such actions have been disregarded by higher levels of government (23/02/21 P19).

Narratives recount that during the initial stages of the refugee crisis on the island, the local community demonstrated remarkable unity and provided assistance to refugees. However, as the years have elapsed, a sense of fatigue has permeated the inhabitants, leading to a collective desire for the relocation of the Reception and Identification Center (RIC) from the island. This sentiment persists despite the narrative's acknowledgment that the community derives some financial benefits from the RIC (01/12/20 P6). Notably, in specific locales like Xyrokambos, residents exhibit a negative stance toward asylum seekers (01/12/20 P7). As per a narrative, the municipal authority, having presided since 2011 and undergoing its third term during the interviews, undertook responsibilities during what is described as 'the most challenging post-war period', marked by various difficulties, notably the substantial issue of migrant refugees. Among the challenges highlighted is the circumstance that refugees, upon obtaining asylum, are expected to depart from the island due to the limited employment opportunities in Leros as a small island. Nevertheless, the narrative conveys that a considerable number of individuals who secure asylum still continue to reside on the island, inhabiting older structures. This tendency persists either because of a reluctance to leave the familiar locale or due to a lack of means for relocation (23/02/21 P19). Local actors assert that the recently established a new Closed Controlled Structure for asylum seekers is causing an environmental calamity on the island. Notably, the specific area has been officially designated as a historical site by gazette through the Ministry of Culture. Described as an arbitrary construction, the narrative emphasizes a significant failure to adhere to the island's environmental and urban planning conditions during the facility's construction phase (09/03/21 P22).

European Union (EU)–Turkey statement: its impact on the RIC of Leros

Local actors consistently assert that the EU–Turkey Agreement has proven ineffective since its inception. One significant repercussion of this ineffectuality manifests when individuals, ineligible for asylum and unable to be deported to Turkey due to its refusal to accept them (01/12/20 P6; 09/05/21 P28), receive a rejection decision. In such cases, these individuals are granted the liberty to depart the RIC and relocate freely, as expressed in the narrative, «to go wherever they happen to be, they just let them go» (01/12/20 P6). The impediment to deportation to Turkey results in a prolonged stay on the islands for those awaiting a subsequent rejection decision, with the initial refusal leading to their detainment by the police and placement at pre-removal detention centers without onward transit to Turkey (09/05/21 P28). An additional account underscores that the impact of the EU–Turkey Agreement is predominantly reflected in its consequences for both the islands and the nation at large. This agreement directly contributes to the protracted presence of asylum seekers on the islands, extending to those who have received an unfavorable asylum decision. Particularly noteworthy is the alteration in the asylum landscape for Syrian refugees. In contrast to the past, where Syrians were expeditiously granted asylum, the agreement designates Turkey as a 'safe third country' for the return of Syrians, thereby precluding them from obtaining asylum in Greece (23/02/21 P19). These narratives reveal a violation of individuals' right to a fair assessment of their asylum requests as outlined in the 1951 Geneva Convention on the Status of Refugees and its 1967 Protocol. As a result, the localization of human rights within this context faces an imminent threat, leading to the deterioration of human rights at the grassroots level.

Conflicts of interest in Leros: the local society has been 'divided'

While one narrative presents Leros as cohesive, with a shared goal for the RIC to generate local employment and counter external influence (23/02/21 P19), the prevailing narrative suggests a societal division with a nuanced perspective on the impact of the RIC. Societal divisions arise, particularly among those in tourism who link a decline in tourism to the RIC, contrary to RIC employees citing governmental benefits (22/01/21 P16). Residents, considering the island's nontouristic nature, express positivity about the new RIC structures, anticipating job creation and addressing unemployment (05/09/21 P28). The local government's opposition to the new RIC stems from a reluctance to anchor the island's economy in migration, contradicting the perspective that the RIC would serve as a solution to the prevailing unemployment challenges (09/03/21 P22). While a narrative suggests the local community's familiarity and tolerance for diversity and island structures, this perspective is contingent upon the presence of significant interests and rivalries. Local actors advocate against RICs on the islands, not solely for tourism reasons but also due to the adverse living conditions in closed camps, emphasizing the detrimental effects on both the local residents and stranded asylum seekers in Leros. «Regardless of any potential retributive benefits, Leros has nothing to gain, much less the refugees» (22/01/21 P16).

Metaphors in the narratives about the RIC at Leros

The metaphorical concept of 'entrapment' is invoked within the narrative. The portrayal delineates that the islands persist in a state of being 'trapped', concurrently asserting that 'refugee immigrants also remain trapped' (23/02/21 P19).

This metaphor conveys a nuanced perspective on the conditions affecting both the islands and the refugee immigrants, encapsulating a sense of confinement and limitation. The RIC in Leros is characterized in the narrative as 'another village' necessitating management by local authorities. Described as a 'weight', its substantial scale stands in stark contrast to the petite dimensions of Leros, a notably diminutive island. Within this narrative, the assertion is made that 'a tiny island cannot bear such a great burden' (23/02/21 P19). It is underscored that the EU needs to comprehend that the islands are not merely a 'repository of souls' (09/03/21 P22). It is emphasized in the narrative that there are currently 'millions of souls' on the islands due to the EU's lack of readiness to manage immigration and its insufficient support to Greece (05/09/21 P28). The local community endeavors to forestall the transformation of the island into a 'hell' by opposing the relocation of asylum seekers from other islands, such as Lesvos. They adamantly reject the island being 'stigmatized' once more, reminiscent of historical instances involving the mentally ill or other vulnerable groups. According to the narrative, the predicament of RICs is not localized to the host islands but is deemed 'national, pan-European and global'. Consequently, the narrative posits that the 'burden' should be a shared responsibility and each entity should 'bear the burden' proportionately (23/02/21 P19).

Leros, while having 'embraced' numerous diversities, finds itself unable to endure being relegated 'on the sidelines'. An emergent 'industry' surrounding immigration is taking shape on the island. Leros contends with a 'prolonged crisis', marked by a state of being 'marginalized' due to immigration and the RIC exerts adverse effects on the local tourism sector. RIC is leaving an adverse 'print' and 'stamp' on the island's narrative. The deliberate influx of a substantial number of immigrants is described as 'loading' the border, constituting a 'dangerous mistake' with implications at the national level. Particularly for the 'frontline' islands situated on the border, the RIC is perceived as an instigator of a national disaster (09/03/21 P22).

Narratives underscore the presence of domestic violence and drug trafficking within the RIC, contributing to the portrayal of these facilities as opaque 'black boxes'. This characterization stems from the challenge of attributing responsibility, thereby complicating the administration of justice. Notably, the Leros police have explicitly indicated their lack of jurisdiction in addressing incidents of violence occurring within the confines of the RIC (01/12/20 P6). RIC is metaphorically paralleled to prisons, prompting a poignant question from a local actor: «*would you like to live in front of a prison?*» The RIC is a negative 'page in the history' of Leros, while in this narrative, the residents of the island harbor a reluctance to assume a status akin to 'Lebenduza' (09/03/21 P22).

8 Lesvos, Moria until September 2020 and Mavrovouni or Kara Tepe

On Lesvos, a RIC (Reception and Identification Center)/hotspot was operating in Moria which burned down in September 2020, and thus the accommodation structure in Kara Tepe was created. The official capacity of the RIC in Moria was 2,840 people, but in 2019 the number of asylum seekers reached 20,785, while after the fire in Moria, in 2020 there were 9,189 asylum seekers residing in the Kara Tepe structure (Ministry of Immigration and Asylum, annual report 12/2020). At the time of the interviews, there were two accommodation structures, one RIC in Kara Tepe (or otherwise Mavrovouni) and one accommodation structure in PIKPA. On October 31, 2020, it was decided to transfer the 100 immigrants from the PIKPA that houses the Neapolis structure. Lesbos has a total population of 85,330 inhabitants (Hellenic Statistical Authority, 2011 census) and the municipality of Mytilini has a population of 37,890 inhabitants (Hellenic Statistical Authority, 2011 census). At the time of the interviews, the mayor of the municipality of Mytilini was Stratis Kytelis with the combination 'Strength of Unity in the Municipality of Mytilini'. Moreover, the municipal council of the municipality consists of the factions 'Allazoume ton topo mas', 'Me pyksida ton politi', 'Laiki Syspeirosi Mytilinis Municipality', 'Epanekkinisiv and 'Lesvos opos tis aksizei'.

Empirical research on the RIC of Moria and Mavrovouni, Lesvos

The RIC in Moria has been characterized by actors' narratives as «the whole thing was a challenge» (11/03/21 P23) and when it started to expand no one could predict how it was going to develop. Local actors delineate that during the summer of 2015, an influx of approximately 1,500–2,000 individuals daily was observed in Moria. According to local actors, it started with a population of around 800 residents and reached around 25,000 people shortly before it burned down in September 2020 (11/03/21 P23/13/11/20 P1), occupying an area of 220 hectares. Narratives underscore the financial magnitude of the Moria RIC, costing 8 million euros and inaugurated in 2015, operative until its untimely cessation in September 2020 due to a destructive conflagration.

Following the incident, the RIC underwent a transient relocation to a private sector in Mavrovouni or Kara Tepe. As of the interview period in March 2021, the population of asylum seekers residing in Mavrovouni numbered fewer than 7,000.

DOI: 10.4324/9781003468134-12

Simultaneously, municipal Kara Tepe, a municipal establishment hosting 1,600 asylum seekers, is characterized by local actors as 'excellent' and deemed the most meticulously organized center in Lesvos (11/03/21 P23; 13/11/20 P1). An additional contingent of 700 individuals resided in domiciles facilitated by the ESTIA housing program for vulnerable asylum seekers on the island. Subsequent to the decision to cease ESTIA operations on the islands, plans were established to transfer asylum seekers to Mavrovouni. Analogously, a parallel course of events transpired with the accommodation facility for asylum seekers and refugees in PIKPA, extolled by local actors as a 'dignified structure' (11/03/21 P23; 13/11/20 P1).

In Moria, an estimated 6,000–7,000 asylum seekers were housed within the structured confines of the official Registration and Identification Center (RIC), while the remainder resided in the periphery of the designated center. Accounts from within the RIC depict the existence of 'unfortunate conditions' and 'chaos'; notwithstanding, efforts were made to provide informal education and avenues for creative employment for children. These initiatives were made possible through the contribution and support of individuals dedicated to solidarity who actively participated in delivering these services. Conversely, outside the official RIC, specifically in the area referred to by local actors as the 'Olive Grove', a marked distinction prevailed. Unlike the structured environment of the official reception center with its containers, the 'Olive Grove' lacked such accommodations. Approximately 18,000 individuals inhabited this space, residing in tents or makeshift huts, contending with exceedingly challenging living conditions.

Challenges in the RICs of Lesvos (Moria and Mavrovouni)

The RIC in Moria emerges in the narratives of various local actors as a complex entity embodying 'two different things at the same time'. On one facet lies the organized RIC, while on the other, an informal settlement, colloquially referred to as a 'slum', materialized outside the official RIC perimeter. According to narratives, the primary challenges within the official RIC encompassed the cohabitation of diverse individuals amidst arduous conditions, the provision of elementary health services and the subpar quality of sustenance – an aspect confirmed through a municipal council investigation prompting an appeal to the prosecutor (11/03/21 P23). The imperative need for hundreds of children within the RIC to experience a semblance of normalcy, entailing access to education and opportunities for creative engagement, was underscored. Narratives further underscored the pervasive challenges arising from the substantial population residing in the RIC, manifesting in struggles to secure decent living conditions and fulfill basic needs pertaining to sustenance, clothing and bedding (30/11/20 P5). Additional challenges revolved around protracted waiting times for essential services such as food and medical attention, alongside concerns about sanitation, incidents of violence and the protection of minor children within the RIC structure. The actors directly invoked the children's right to education, emphasizing the obligation to safeguard this right, given the absence of educational opportunities for children residing in the RIC (11/13/20 P1). Moreover, the narratives articulated the right to food in connection with the right against inhumane treatment, establishing a direct link to children's entitlements to education and play.

Beyond the confines of the RIC, as per the narratives of local actors, the predominant challenge manifested in the arduous 'housing' conditions. Notably, the 'Olive Grove' presented a host of challenges due to the absence of distinct segregation among its populace, distinguishing it from the structured organization within the official RIC (11/13/20 P1; 30/11/20 P5; 11/03/21 P23). Consequently, unaccompanied minors, families and individual adults coexisted within the same spatial confines. Within this setting, opportunistic groups emerged, seeking to exploit asylum seekers by proffering promises of securing essential documents for departure from the RIC. Simultaneously, the 'Olive Grove' encountered a spectrum of issues, ranging from thefts to conflicts among disparate ethnic groups and even instances of intimidation and threats posed by distinct ethnic gangs. This complex environment posed multifaceted challenges, necessitating a nuanced understanding of the dynamics at play outside the official RIC (11/03/21 P23).

In September 2020, the Moria RIC burned down, leading to the relocation of asylum seekers to Mavrovouni (also informally known as Kara Tepe). While the Ministry of Migration Policy asserts improved conditions in Mavrovouni compared to Moria, local actors dispute this claim. Mavrovouni, where the RIC was situated when the interviews were conducted, is susceptible to extreme weather conditions, resulting in flooding. Additionally, the electricity supply is inadequate, with only 5–6 hours of availability each day (11/03/21 P23; 13/11/20 P1; 30/11/20 P5). Despite the provision of blankets and clothes, there is no heating. Local actors emphasize that, based on measurements, residents of Mavrovouni have an average of about 7 minutes of hot water per person per week for bathing. Moreover, an additional challenge arises from the restriction on solidarity groups entering the RIC area for the transportation of goods. Consequently, groups such as 'Coexistence and Communication in the Aegean' provide essential items at the entrance, allowing internal distribution. Simultaneously, local actors offering assistance remain uninformed about the ongoing situation within the RIC. In Mavrovouni, the absence of a dedicated facility for vulnerable women and single-parent families is notable. However, a positive development involves the relocation of all minors from the RIC to the hinterland, addressing this specific concern (11/13/20 P1).

Local narratives delve into the intricate dynamics within the Registration and Identification Center (RIC), an environment markedly shaped by national government policies, particularly influenced by the implementation of the Dublin I and Dublin II Treaties. These treaties dictate that the 'country of first reception' assumes the responsibility of processing asylum requests (11/03/21 P23; 13/11/20 P1). However, local narratives highlight a discernible contradiction, as Greece, being the primary country of first reception, witnesses a reluctance among refugees to seek asylum within its borders. According to the account of a local actor, the living conditions within the RIC, specifically in Mavrovouni and even more so in Moria, are deemed 'not at all decent and adequate'. Within this narrative, the RIC is portrayed as transcending the scope of municipal responsibility. The narrative delves into the ramifications of the RIC on the local community, elucidating its implications for the rights of the local populace. It underscores the municipality's obligation to safeguard the rights and interests of its residents (26/03/21 P25).

Challenges in Lesvos due to the existence of the RICs at Moria and Mavrovouni

In Lesvos, local actors highlight a multifaceted challenge related to the RIC, revealing diverse reactions among residents. A complex narrative emerges as some residents, albeit a minority but with vocal expressions, call for the departure of asylum seekers, stating phrases like 'kick them out' and expressing a reluctance to have them in the area due to perceived unemployment issues. In contrast, a segment of the local population exhibits sincere solidarity with refugees (11/30/20 P5).

Concurrently, the presence of the RIC yields substantial economic benefits for various residents, particularly those who lease their properties in proximity to the facility, such as in Mytilini, Panagiouda and Pamphila. This economic gain is attributed to the significant number of individuals settling on the island, including workers from organizations like the UN High Commission, United Nations International Children's Emergency Fund, the International Organization for Migration (IOM), government officials from the Ministry of Migration Policy, FRONTEX personnel and NGO (nongovernmental organization) workers and volunteers. The population settling on the island typically resides in rented accommodations or hotels, fostering economic activities such as restaurants catering exclusively to this demographic. Notably, this economic influence is predominantly concentrated in the vicinity of Mytilini.

Before the fire in Moria, there was public desire for the camp to relocate, but posttransfer to Mavrovouni, locals faced economic losses (11/13/2020 P1). The identified challenges encompass multifaceted issues, including sanitation concerns, assaults orchestrated by far-right factions targeting both advocates of solidarity and refugees. Notably, the formation of assault battalions in Moria assumed quasi-authoritative roles as 'police' and 'justice', dictating citizen movements and perpetrating violence against NGO personnel en route to refugee locations. Furthermore, a local tension surfaces concerning the educational provision for refugee children, exacerbated by the resistance within a segment of the local society towards integrating refugee children into the educational infrastructure on the island (11/13/2020 P1; 11/30/20 P5; 11/03/21 P23). In a similar vein, a narrative underscores a humanitarian crisis ensuing from an abrupt influx of people, causing social cohesion issues and internal tensions within the local community. The incident significantly impacted the society of Mytilene and the broader island. Initially, the local community exhibited commendable solidarity and humanitarian support, even amid a national economic crisis. This unique and remarkable response waned as the escalating number of asylum seekers on the island, driven by European Union policies, created weariness among the local populace. The sudden surge in population, combined with the confinement of around 20,000 individuals in adverse living conditions, resulted in delinquency and disruptive behavior. Consequently, an atmosphere of insecurity, disturbance and internal division emerged among the local community regarding the appropriate treatment of refugees (11/03/21 P23). An alternative narrative emphasizes the challenges faced by the municipality in administrative, social and economic aspects due to the increased bureaucratic workload and strained resources. This narrative accentuates the imposition of a burden on the city due to asylum seekers circulating within urban areas, consequently amplifying the demands placed on municipal resources. The exigencies generated by the RIC on the island manifest an imbalance vis-à-vis the funding allocated to the municipality. The dissonance arises from the necessity to engage in tenders, submit funding applications and partake in National Strategic Reference Framework (NSRF) programs, all of which necessitate additional resources beyond the current fiscal provisions.The narrative underscores the need for support and solidarity to address these challenges, focusing on the impact on the citizens of Lesvos and their social and cultural identity (26/03/21 P25).

European Union (EU)–Turkey statement: its impact on the RIC of Lesvos

In the account of the local political leadership, the municipality, by virtue of its institutional limitations, refrains from adjudicating the EU–Turkey Agreement. Both administratively and politically, the municipality maintains a nonparticipatory stance in this agreement, asserting its lack of institutional engagement. Consequently, the local actor is constrained from expressing an opinion on the agreement's success or ramifications, deeming it a domain 'outside the boundaries' of the municipality. In adherence to this perspective, the municipal authority abstains from engaging in the discourse surrounding the EU–Turkey Agreement, deeming this abstention as 'doing the right thing'. The municipality asserts its circumscribed role, confined to the immediate management of local societal issues (26/03/21 P25).

Conversely, divergent narratives held by various local actors posit that the EU–Turkey Agreement exerts a palpable influence on the societal fabric of Lesvos. The agreement introduces intricate bureaucratic procedures and an operational mechanism perceived as beyond the EU's effective oversight. Local narratives pivot towards the democratic shortfall within Turkey, characterizing it as a barrier to fostering a cooperative relationship with the country. The agreement's direct consequence, manifested through the imposition of 'geographical limitation' and the provision for on-island examination of asylum claims, culminates in the concentration of the asylum-seeking population in the Aegean region. This concentration, resulting from the surge in asylum claims, insufficient staffing within asylum services and a lack of expedited claims processing assistance from the EU, creates a humanitarian crisis. Concurrently, the influx of the population continues unabated, heightening the strain on resources and exacerbating the crisis (11/03/21 P23; 13/11/20 P1; 30/11/20 P5). Consequently, the indirect consequence of the Agreement becomes evident as it contributes to the humanitarian crisis, driven by the inadvertent entrapment of asylum seekers on the islands (11/03/21 P23). In this context, the agreement exerts a discernible influence on refugee solidarity, detrimentally affecting their well-being. Within the framework of the glocalization of human rights, the prospects for the actualization of human rights are diminished.

Conflicts of interest in Lesvos: economic benefit and public discourse

Local narratives on Lesvos reveal a dual dynamic. Some benefit economically from the RIC, while others express discontent over perceived damages and tourism decline. Conflicting interests exist with minimal overt tensions. Another narrative highlights an oxymoronic scenario, where those financially profiting from the RIC publicly oppose refugees (11/13/20 P1; 11/03/ 21 P23).

In an alternative local narrative, the absence of divergent interests within the local community is posited. Societally, the adverse impacts of immigration on the local community are deemed incalculable and uncompensatable. The purported economic benefits attributed to immigration, particularly from the RIC, do not, in this perspective, outweigh the negative repercussions, including the tarnishing of the island's reputation. Arguments asserting financial gains and urging local satisfaction are deemed ethically questionable in this narrative. According to this narrative, the island did not intentionally adopt an economic model predicated on immigration, nor has profiting from the global plight ever constituted an objective for the local community (26/03/21 P25).

In an alternative narrative, a semblance of congruence emerges in interests, as both the local community and the asylum seekers accommodated in the RIC Tex-press a shared aversion. The inhabitants of the RIC harbor no desire to be present on the island, mirroring the sentiment of the local community in Lesvos, which opposes the establishment of the structure on their soil. Simultaneously, the local community perceives that the involvement of various NGOs indirectly encourages the influx of additional asylum seekers to the island. Despite potential disparities in perspectives among NGO workers, volunteers, asylum seekers and the local community, a prevailing commonality exists – a shared interest in expeditiously resolving the presence of the RIC structure on the island (30/11/20 P5).

Metaphors in the narratives about the RIC at Lesvos

In a local narrative, both the RIC in Mavrovouni and notably Moria are metaphorically denoted as 'the shame of Europe'. This metaphorical expression implies a moral condemnation, characterizing the RICs as disgraceful and reflecting negatively on Europe as a whole. However, the oversight and management of the RIC operations, as well as the conditions prevailing within, are expressly stated not to fall within the purview of the municipal authority (26/03/21 P25).

Another narrative employs a metaphor to accentuate the European Union's substantial financial commitment aimed at preventing refugee influx across Greece's borders. According to this account, the EU demonstrates a willingness to allocate substantial funds for the establishment of what is metaphorically characterized as 'ultra-luxurious concentration camps'. This metaphor evokes a historical comparison to concentration camps, suggesting a critical view of the proposed facilities.

The situation is marked by the forced retention of refugees within Greece, notwithstanding their expressed desire to move elsewhere, all justified under the banner of human rights, as per the narrative (11/03/21 P23).

The sudden transformation of the island of Lesvos into a host of a 'second big city' is metaphorically underscored, wherein either Moria or the current Mavrovouni serves as the surrogate refugee city alongside the island's primary settlement with 30,000 inhabitants. This metaphor implies a significant and abrupt change in the island's demographics and social dynamics. Within this paradigm, the narrative delineates the erosion of societal solidarity, describing sentiments that metaphorically convey a sense of helplessness, indifference and emotional fatigue. Expressions like 'I don't care anymore' and 'we can't do it anymore, do what you understand, I can't stand it' metaphorically depict the societal response to the challenges posed by the refugee situation, suggesting a breakdown in collective resilience and compassion (11/03/21 P23).

The main narrative highlights that the prevailing sentiment among the majority of the local community of Lesvos, as of the interviews conducted in March 2021, leans against endorsing expansive structures, particularly concerning the proposed Closed Controlled Structure. The opposition to large structures is metaphorically framed as resistance against the envisioned establishment. The community, within this metaphorical framework, expresses support for a compact registration structure designed for asylum seekers with a brief intended stay of a few days. However, it adamantly rejects the notion of establishing a 'camp' where tens of thousands of refugees would be metaphorically 'imprisoned', residing at a considerable remove from the broader social fabric. The term 'imprisoned' is employed metaphorically to underscore the perceived isolating and segregating nature of such large-scale refugee accommodations (11/03/21 P23).

Within the prevailing discourse, the envisioned Closed Controlled Structures slated for establishment on each island are metaphorically and ironically cast as expansive, contemporary facilities endowed with 'all the comforts'. This figurative language insinuates a purposeful and ironic portrayal of these structures, accentuating their extensive amenities with the intention of compelling all incoming refugees to remain within their confines. These grandiose 'superstructures', designed to house 5,000 or more individuals, are metaphorically likened to the emblematic imagery of expansive camps located outside Lebanon, accommodating millions of refugees. Notably, the term 'concentration camps' is introduced, serving as a metaphorical descriptor that underscores their character as protracted-stay accommodations rather than mere identification facilities. The opposition to the establishment of these substantial structures is principally rooted in three key rationales, as elucidated in the narrative. Firstly, there exists a hesitancy to steer the trajectory of the islands towards hosting 'large refugee camps', a concept viewed as incompatible with an island inhabited by 100,000 people. Secondly, the refugees themselves express a desire not to linger on Lesvos. Thirdly, the proposed centers face criticism as potential 'ghettos' due to their remote positioning from populated areas, cultivating an environment where refugees are distanced from local society, lacking opportunities for integration and education. This critique is underpinned by the acknowledgment that such seclusion runs counter to the rights accorded to the refugee population under international conventions. This nuanced perspective is explicitly emphasized in the narrative, highlighting the reliance on metaphorical expressions to convey complex viewpoints (11/03/21 P23).

The EU–Turkey Agreement, initially hailed but eventually deemed 'flaky', is metaphorically depicted as an accord 'built on sand', symbolizing its fragile foundation and subsequent abrupt collapse. This portrayal emphasizes the perceived failure of the agreement and the consequential confinement it imposed, characterizing it as 'disastrous' for the island, thereby underscoring the negative repercussions associated with this diplomatic initiative (11/03/21 P23). The citizens of Mytilene assume a metaphorical 'target of criticism', oscillating between portrayals as embodiments of solidarity and occasional suggestions of harboring racist sentiments. This figurative characterization serves strategic purposes in advancing distinct agendas. Positioned 'on the back of the Mytilene citizen', who contends with the weariness induced by fluctuating opinions and policies resulting in various societal 'labels', the local community, initially supportive of asylum seekers, eventually succumbs to fatigue. The narrative underscores the inherent unfairness of passing judgment and 'pointing the finger' at the citizens of Mytilene, urging consideration of their unique circumstances amid an unprecedented influx of 20,000 immigrants and refugees into the city. Moreover, the narrative draws attention to instances where other European countries face criticism for rejecting a small number of refugees, highlighting a contrast with the repeated censure faced by the local community of Mytilene despite accommodating a significant refugee population. Within this framework, residents of Mytilini assert that, unlike other citizens defending their municipalities, they perceive a lack of solidarity toward their own, contributing to administrative challenges within the municipality (26/03/21 P25).

The narrative accentuates that individuals residing within the RIC are metaphorically characterized as 'not imprisoned', emphasizing their freedom to venture outside and move about the city. This metaphorical portrayal, however, introduces an additional burden as the needs of the city escalate, particularly during a period when an additional 20,000 individuals availed themselves of municipal services. Within the same narrative, incidents of petty theft are acknowledged, yet the absence of significant problems related to violence or crime mitigates personal frictions with the local community. Instead, the narrative suggests that frictions predominantly manifest in the realm of human rights. The living conditions are akin to those in Moria, where families endure circumstances described as residing in the 'mud' and facing 'tragic conditions' exacerbated by adverse weather phenomena, particularly impact children. The narrative contends that such conditions violate the rights of refugees and immigrants, presenting a stark contrast to the cultural values attributed to Mytilene, Europe and the local populace. The locals, it is asserted, experience distress when coexisting with individuals whose rights are compromised, thereby emphasizing the centrality of human rights concerns within the community. A narrative employs metaphors to illustrate the dual violation of human rights, referring to the complex dynamics and challenges faced by both the refugee population and the citizens of the local community on the island of Lesvos. The local citizens are metaphorically described as being 'pressured', unable to claim what is due to them for their municipality, creating a sense of constraint and limitation in pursuing their civic needs. The absence of a closed swimming pool, which is framed as a basic amenity, becomes symbolic of the disparities and discontinuity between the needs of the local community and the refugees residing on Lesbos. A metaphorical weight is attributed to Lesvos, encompassing social, administrative and economic dimensions, creating an 'unequal burden' that hinders the progress and prosperity of Mytilene compared to other cities in Greece and Europe. The island is portrayed as lagging behind and the citizens of Mytilene, despite being European, are metaphorically depicted as lacking the same opportunities and perspectives as their counterparts in more prosperous cities (26/03/21 P25).

The injustice faced by the inhabitants of Lesvos is emphasized, highlighting the violation of human rights within this context. The narrative advocates for the acknowledgment of this injustice at the level of human rights discourse, urging a nuanced understanding that goes beyond comparative arguments such as economic disparities or worse conditions in other regions. The metaphorical plea is to ensure that the concerns of the local citizens are heard and addressed, even as the predominant public discourse tends to emphasize the rights of refugees. The narrative underscores the need for a balanced approach that acknowledges and addresses the rights of both the refugee population and the citizens of the local community.

9 Samos, Vathy

Samos consists of the municipality of Eastern Samos with its seat in the city of Samos and the municipality of West Samos with its seat in Karlovasi. The RIC (Reception and Identification Center) of Samos is located in the municipal unit of Vatheos which belongs to the municipality of Eastern Samos. The official capacity of the RIC in Vathi at Samos was 648 people, but in 2019 the number of asylum seekers residing in the island structure reached 8,064 people, and in 2020, there were 3,556 asylum seekers residing in the structure (Ministry of Immigration and Asylum, annual report 12/2020). Samos has a total population of 32,974 inhabitants (Hellenic Statistical Authority, 2011 census) and the municipality of Eastern Samos has a population of 22,654 inhabitants (Hellenic Statistical Authority, 2011 census). At the time of the interviews, the mayor of the municipality of Eastern Samos was Georgios Stanzos with the municipal association 'ANA.S.A. for Samos'.

Empirical research on the RIC of Vathy, Samos

The distinctive feature of the Samos RIC is its integration within the urban fabric of Samos, a departure from the typical configuration of RICs on other islands, which are situated approximately 15 minutes away by car. While Samos experienced modest refugee flows from 2000 to 2010, the influx of asylum seekers surged dramatically in 2015. Initially, during the onset of heightened migration flows in 2015, a significant number of Samos residents actively contributed, such as by providing breakfast assistance. However, following the implementation of the EU–Turkey Agreement and a subsequent substantial increase in the number of asylum seekers to approximately 8,000 individuals, the dynamics shifted. This surge overwhelmed the capacity of the RIC and strained the provision of services within the facility.

Challenges in the RIC of Samos

The predominant challenges within the RIC of Samos are underscored by inhumane and degrading living conditions (25/11/20 P4) and the persistent issue of overpopulation (08/03/21 P21; 25/11/20 P4; 12/03/21 P24; 19/11/20 P3; 22/12/20 P11; 18/11/20 P2), resulting in a compromised ability to establish and enforce essential rules (12/03/21 P24). The Samos facility, originally designed for 600 occupants,

DOI: 10.4324/9781003468134-13

experienced an alarming surge to accommodate 4,000 individuals, surpassing historical figures of 8,000–8,500 residents in the RIC (21/01/21 P14). The narrative highlights the narrative intention of 'incarcerating' asylum seekers on the islands as a strategic measure to dissuade further refugee inflow (03/08/21 P21). Confrontations arising from religious and ethnic differences among asylum seekers also emerge as significant challenges within the RIC (03/08/21 P21; 25/11/20 P4).

The portrayal of living conditions in the RIC on Samos is starkly characterized as 'unacceptable' and 'miserable'. As winter sets in, asylum seekers primarily residing outside the official RIC endure exposure to harsh elements, residing amidst mud and cold. Tent availability is constrained, especially for those setting up in forested and privately owned areas, as encroachment restrictions limit United Nations International Children's Emergency Fund tent provisions (25/11/20 P4). The adverse living conditions extend to the unauthorized tent settlements in olive and pine trees, colloquially referred to as the 'jungle' by field activists (19/11/20 P3; 22/12/20 P11). The asylum seekers found themselves in a state of isolation, devoid of support from established state structures. Faced with the overwhelming overpopulation within the RIC and acting always under the guidance of the officers of the RIC (25/11/20 P4), asylum seekers were compelled to establish makeshift living arrangements. These arrangements extended beyond the confines of the official RIC, prompting them to pitch tents amidst olive and pine trees in the peripheral 'jungle', a term coined by field actors (19/11/20 P3; 22/12/20 P11). This makeshift settlement extended to private properties, involving the cutting down of olive trees and the repurposing of abandoned houses to create improvised dwellings. This initiative aimed to shield them from the protracted exposure to hazardous weather conditions. Notably, this makeshift settlement in the 'jungle' accommodated vulnerable populations, including families with newborns, pregnant women, unaccompanied minors and individuals with disabilities (25/11/20 P4; 22/12/20 P11).

An additional formidable challenge, as articulated by a narrative, underscores the stark deficiency of supportive structures on Samos for vulnerable groups. The absence of structures is exemplified by the discontinuation of programs. Following the cessation of this program, a substantial population within vulnerable groups contends with an absence of assistance. Another prominent challenge that compounds the complexities faced by Samos is the prevalence of violence within the RIC. A distressing aspect of this violence is evident in cases of sexual assault victims confined within the RIC, who are compelled to coexist with their perpetrators due to the unavailability of hostels to shelter these victims (25/11/20 P4).

The adverse ramifications of a concentrated refugee/immigrant population and their prolonged presence on the island manifest in various detrimental consequences. Service provision is strained, exemplified by understaffed facilities, notably evident in the sole presence of one doctor within the RIC (19/11/20 P3; 25/11/20 P4). A critical concern surfaces in the realm of healthcare, with challenges in upholding the right to health due to limited medical personnel. The imperative to safeguard the well-being of refugee children and uphold their right to education emerges as a pressing request within this context (08/03/2021 P21). The adverse living conditions extend beyond the RIC, particularly in the 'jungle' area, where hygiene complications compound the perilous environment. The prevalence of unsanitary conditions, abundant weeds and an overall lack of cleanliness contribute to an environment described as ‘dirty’. Residents endure exposure to the harsh cold and grapple with psychological trauma, emphasizing the multifaceted challenges faced by individuals inhabiting this area (11/19/20 P3).

A significant challenge is intricately linked to the inherent difficulty in formulating long-term objectives due to the constant flux of data. This challenge is exacerbated by legislative changes that intensify the complexity of the asylum-seeking process, particularly for individuals lacking proficiency in the Greek language and facing difficulties comprehending legal terminology and mandated time frames (18/11/20 P2; 19/11/20 P3; 25/11/20 P4; 08/03/21 P21). The intricacies of the process are further compounded by the documentation of decisions in Greek, presenting a formidable hurdle for asylum seekers. Notably, interpretation services are only provided during the stage where individuals are apprised of the grounds for their rejection and subsequent return to Turkey (25/11/20 P4).

Challenges in Samos due to the existence of the RIC at Vathy

In the island of Samos, initial solidarity from the local community toward refugees was apparent; however, the enactment of the EU–Turkey Agreement in 2015 and subsequent border closures precipitated a rapid surge in the asylum seeker population on Samos, reaching up to 8,000 individuals from an initial 600–700. This surge led to the emergence of makeshift settlements within the city, colloquially termed ‘favelas’, contributing to a growing sense of alienation within the local community. While the far-right organization Samos SOS made its presence known during this period, it did not instigate extreme situations akin to those observed on Lesvos. Although RICs on the islands are typically not positioned within urban centers, the RIC in Samos was initially situated within the confines of the city of Samos. Throughout the course of the field research and interviews conducted, it became evident that there were plans to establish a new Closed Controlled Centre at Zervos, a location situated outside the city center, approximately 20 minutes away. This proposed site, described by some as being ‘in the middle of nowhere’ (25/11/20 P4), signifies a deliberate move away from the urban center. In the local narrative, the demographic imbalance, with periods featuring 5,000 locals alongside 8,000 refugees, raised concerns even among well-intentioned individuals, as state structures failed to provide the necessary support. The existence of the RICs on the islands drew international attention and condemnation. According to accounts, the government engaged in what is described as ‘extortion’ of asylum seekers on the island, an act perceived as a ‘brutal’ form of blackmail against the local community. This assertion is supported by the sustained high population numbers within the RIC, remaining consistently elevated despite fluctuations (e.g., 07/07/19: 3,450 asylum seekers/08/03/21: 3,440 asylum seekers) (08/03/21 P21).

The placement of the RIC within the city of Samos presents a dual narrative, embodying positive implications for asylum seekers and simultaneously generating negative repercussions for the local population. The advantageous aspect lies in the asylum seekers' proximity to urban amenities, fostering the exercise of their right to movement and easy access to city facilities, thereby positively influencing their psychological well-being. However, this spatial arrangement raises concerns for the local inhabitants, as there is a notable absence of initiatives to acquaint them with the asylum seekers, rendering the local population ostensibly 'helpless' in the face of these dynamics.

Compounding these challenges is the issue of environmental impact, characterized by a persistent stench emanating from the waste generated by the RIC. This environmental concern is exacerbated by the reported absence of additional financial assistance to the municipality for comprehensive cleaning efforts. Simultaneously, the island contends with substantial challenges, notably within its understaffed public services such as hospitals, police and prosecution authorities. The strain on these services, heightened by the demands of the burgeoning population, leads to malfunctions and further contributes to an atmosphere of discontent.

In this complex context, a noteworthy consequence is the cultivation of animosity toward asylum seekers and individuals associated with the RIC. The grievances manifest in acts of hostility, extending to the physical targeting of NGO (nongovernmental organization) employees and volunteers. Instances of violence, such as the burning of an NGO's vehicle and the pelting of stones at a residence housing volunteers, underscore the palpable tensions and challenges faced by both the local and refugee communities on the island (11/25/20 P4).

After the EU–Turkey Agreement, similar to other islands, when the number of asylum seekers increased to 8,000 people, far exceeding the capacity of the RIC and the services provided within it, there was a shortage of staff in the structure, insufficient facilities in the hospital, a rise in petty thefts and a decrease in tourism. Inside the RIC, located in a residential area, there were incidents of fires. While the island's inhabitants were initially united, after five years, they grew 'tired' – not because they are bad people, but because they feel 'abandoned' and ignored by the EU and the Greek government (19/11/20 P3).

One of the narratives underlines that tourism in Samos has been significantly impacted since the onset of the refugee crisis in 2015–2016, with Vathy perceived as 'tragically' affected, creating concerns about the refugees' movements hindering normal activities, such as visits to playgrounds. The presence of the RIC has altered Samos' identity as a tourist destination, shifting attention from the economy to issues surrounding refugees and immigrants (12/03/21 P24). Contrary narratives debate whether tourism was already in decline due to economic challenges, with an opposing view asserting that Vathy has experienced a rejuvenation facilitated by the refugee population. This rejuvenation is marked by increased market consumption, heightened rental activity and a boost to the hospitality sector (25/11/20 P4). A formidable challenge arose on the islands with the proposal for a new Closed Controlled Structure intended for asylum seekers, designed to house up to 3,000 individuals in Samos (25/11/20 P4; 19/11/20 P3; 22/12/20 P11; 18/11/20 P2). This discourse prompted a series of declarations, processions and demonstrations opposing its implementation, while local authorities simultaneously pushed for the closure of the existing facility, advocating the relocation of asylum seekers to the newly proposed structure. The prevailing local sentiment aligns with the stance of 'no structure, direct decongestion from the islands' (11/18/20 P2). Despite local resistance to the establishment of the new structure, it was ultimately enacted in Samos.

EU–Turkey statement: its impact on the RIC of Samos

Turkey strategically manipulates migration flows (03/08/21 P21), a dynamic profoundly shaped by the far-reaching implications of the EU–Turkey Agreement, notably evident in the evolving situation on Samos. Subsequent to this decision, the imposition of a 'geographic restriction' on the islands commenced. Local actors contend that the RIC should serve as a temporary residence for individuals seeking international protection, only until the completion of their asylum claim registration, not until the protracted process of claim examination concludes, which, based on current data, can extend over several years (25/11/20 P4). The repercussions of the Agreement are described as 'tragic', entwining regions on the islands and in Greece, while Europe's stance is deemed inadequately responsive (12/03/21 P24). Moreover, narratives attribute the predicament in the RIC to the EU–Turkey Agreement's impracticalities. The Agreement, in practice, fails to materialize its objectives, with the asylum service ill-equipped to manage the overwhelming volume of requests. The absence of effective returns to Turkey results in individuals enduring dire conditions on the island for extended periods, creating a state of impasse (19/11/20 P3).

Additionally, in the same line with the narratives in Leros, the EU–Turkey Agreement contributes to a significant number of rejected asylum applications, particularly affecting asylum seekers, predominantly from Syria, who have transited through Turkey. During interviews, the focus shifts from the safety of their home country, Syria, to inquiries about their experiences in Turkey, emphasizing their capacity to settle in Turkey rather than necessitating migration to Europe (22/12/20 P11). A prominent consequence of the Agreement is the looming risk of refoulement to Turkey, designated as a safe country (11/18/20 P2). These narratives elucidate a transgression of the individuals' entitlement to a judicious examination of their asylum claim in accordance with the provisions set forth in the 1951 Geneva Convention relating to the Status of Refugees and its 1967 Protocol. The procedural scrutiny applied to these claims diverges from the foundational principles espoused by the Geneva Convention. Consequently, within this framework, the glocalization of human rights confronts a looming jeopardy, manifesting in the erosion of human rights at the local level.

Conflicts of interest in Samos: rupture or concord?

In Samos, the presence of the RIC yields economic benefits for specific sectors, such as shops, supermarkets, mini-markets, rental houses and additional police forces. This economic advantage may entail a financial trade-off. However, akin to the sentiments expressed in Leros, the local community adamantly resists anchoring its economic growth in refugee-related activities, firmly rejecting the prospect of deriving profits from the refugee population (03/08/21 P21). Local residents, despite benefiting financially from the refugee presence, express discontent with this economic reliance (11/18/20 P2). In the quotidian affairs of Samos, overt tensions are notably absent, distinguishing it from locales such as Lesvos. Any existing conflicting interests, if present, tend not to manifest prominently in everyday interactions and dynamics (22/12/20 P11). Another narrative posits the absence of a conflict of interest concerning immigration-related turnover, emphasizing the conflict of interest arises only in cases of 'illegitimate' practices, particularly human trafficking, where individuals arriving on the islands are victims. Accordingly, there is a call for the implementation of structured policies aimed at preventing the trafficking of these vulnerable individuals (12/03/21 P24).

A narrative underscores the divergent interests and shared concerns between the local community and asylum seekers on the island. Both factions unequivocally resist the establishment of the RIC and the living conditions imposed on asylum seekers in this challenging environment. Locals, disheartened by the perceived exploitation of the RIC under these adverse circumstances, vehemently reject claims of racism. Their discontent is rooted in a genuine aversion to the difficult conditions asylum seekers endure, reflecting five years of grappling with new challenges on their island. Meanwhile, certain volunteers introduce a relative tension by seizing the opportunity to intertwine volunteering with leisure during study breaks. Despite these dynamics, media accusations depicting locals as racist and unwelcoming to immigrants are fervently contested, as the locals' primary concern lies in the unfavorable living conditions within the RIC rather than animosity toward asylum seekers (19/11/20 P3).

Metaphors in the narratives about the RIC at Samos

A narrative introduces the concept of 'double solidarity' and advocates for the safeguarding of 'double rights'. This metaphorical expression emphasizes the necessity for a dual commitment, encompassing the protection of both the rights of asylum seekers and those of the local community members. On one front, there is an imperative to safeguard the rights of asylum seekers, ensuring the provision of essential goods for them to lead dignified lives in decent conditions. Conversely, the metaphorical 'double right' encapsulates the entitlement of the local community to a sense of security within their environment, underscoring the need for protective measures to address the multifaceted dimensions of rights (03/08/21 P21).

In the portrayed narrative by a local actor, significant financial allocations are metaphorically characterized as 'terrifying amounts', effecting a symbolic transformation of the islands in the eastern Aegean (18/11/20 P2; 19/11/20 P3; 03/08/21 P21; 12/03/21 P24) into what is metaphorically described as 'soul warehouses' (19/11/20 P3; 03/08/21 P21; 12/03/21 P24). A concrete illustration of this considerable expenditure is discernible in the cases of Samos, Leros and Cos, where an auction for the new Closed Controlled Structures absorbed a budget of 120 million euros, complemented by an additional investment of 6,000,000 euros for consulting services from a specific company (03/08/21 P21).

Delving specifically into Samos, the narrative opposes the establishment of a superstructure, namely the Closed Controlled Access Center designed to accommodate over 3,000 asylum seekers. This opposition is grounded in the assertion that Samos, as a border region, encounters logistical challenges in managing such pronounced overpopulation. The narrative forewarns that the introduction of a superstructure would adversely affect tourism and the primary sector, consequently tarnishing the island's image and 'brand name' (03/08/21 P21). The metaphorical depiction of the RIC in Samos is that of leaving a negative 'imprint', necessitating 'reinforced' policies to ameliorate the perceived damage incurred by the locale. The islands, emblematically positioned as a 'bulwark', shoulder the responsibility of managing the refugee influx at a juncture when other European countries display a lack of solidarity and resist sharing these obligations. The narrative suggests that local actors are navigating this complex challenge with a measured approach, articulating a future reluctance to acquiesce to the islands becoming mere 'warehouses' catering to the leisure of 'the North of Europe' (12/03/21 P24).

Part 4

Local narratives and political attitudes

By the discussion outlined in a preceding section (refer to 'Theoretical Framework and Methodology'), when research shifts its focus toward cities as destinations for migration rather than states, ethical considerations regarding migration undergo a distinct transformation. Within this paradigm, political theory necessitates a nuanced examination of cities and states, as cities directly engage with the influx of immigrants, contrasting with the state in its entirety (de Shalit 2018, pp. 1–2). Furthermore, this study adheres to the belief that the effectiveness of political theory relies on its practical application. With this premise serving as its cornerstone, this chapter embraces the framework of 'qualitative political theory' (Cabrera 2009) as its methodological approach.

In this context, diverse theoretical frameworks are applied to analyze the narratives of local actors, thereby establishing connections between these actors' interviews and various theoretical perspectives. Consequently, the integration of these narratives with political theory holds the potential for informing future studies, wherein elements gleaned from actors' narratives contribute to the formulation of arguments within a normative political theory framework (Cabrera 2009). The arguments, metaphors and myths (Gadinger et al. 2019; Freistein et al. 2020; Smith Ochoa et al. 2020) utilized by local actors – such as rural politicians and island professionals in relevant fields – offer insights into the role of human rights specifically at the local level, rather than at the state level as a whole. These narratives are influenced by actors who directly interact with the RIC in their respective locales.

This research adopts the theory that narratives are never neutral (Patterson and Monroe 1998, p. 316). Implicit in this premise is the notion that each narrative espouses principles and values that align more closely with certain ethical approaches and political theories than others. Within this framework, a key inquiry of this study revolves around identifying the moral context at large and the specific political theory to which each actor's narrative pertains. Underlying this inquiry is the acknowledgment that narratives, as constructs aimed at elucidating the complexities of existence, are invariably intertwined with principles that are rooted in moral and political theories. Consequently, each actor's narrative, in its endeavor to 'make sense of the world', is intricately linked to underlying principles, which are in turn embedded within specific moral and political theories. In pursuing this

DOI: 10.4324/9781003468134-14

study's objectives, each narrative offered by various actors will be categorized into broader thematic constructs.

Two primary ethical approaches govern the discourse surrounding the admission of refugees into a country and their rights vis-à-vis the rights and interests of community members. These approaches, namely 'partiality' and 'impartiality', each correspond to distinct currents within political theory. Under the framework of 'partiality', community members are deemed to possess a moral primacy over nonmembers. In this context, states are construed as representatives of their citizenry, thereby justifying the implementation of entry policies aimed at safeguarding and prioritizing the interests of their constituents. Conversely, within the realm of 'impartiality', the rights and interests of community members are regarded with equal weight to those of nonmembers. Hence, policymakers responsible for crafting immigration and entry policies are tasked with balancing the interests and rights of both citizens and foreigners alike. Under the paradigm of 'partiality', states are expected to assume the role of 'cultural communities', whereas in the 'impartiality' approach, states are envisioned to operate as 'cosmopolitan moral actors' (Gibney 2004, pp. 23, 24, 59, 60).

The category of 'impartiality' encompasses currents such as global liberalism, utilitarianism, egalitarianism and libertarian thought, while 'partiality' pertains to political theories such as communitarianism, conservatism and constitutionalism. This book delves into the realm of impartiality, centering its exploration on global liberalism, with a specific examination of the ideas proposed by Carens and on egalitarianism. Within the 'partiality' category, this study will explore conservatism and communitarianism. In this chapter, the two theoretical frameworks from each category will be introduced, accompanied by an examination of their relationship with questions about refugees and the rights and obligations stemming from each theoretical approach. Moreover, a comparative analysis will be undertaken to juxtapose these categories with various rights-based approaches delineated by Miellet (2019), encompassing humanitarian, legal and pragmatic perspectives.

In these contexts, the glocalization of human rights is envisioned through diverse currents. Several theoretical frameworks serve as invaluable aids in conceptualizing localized rights. Concepts rooted in impartiality, notably global liberalism and egalitarianism, offer indispensable guidelines for crafting local policies that prioritize the human rights of vulnerable groups, particularly addressing the well-being of refugees. Conversely, approaches associated with partiality, such as conservatism and communitarianism, exhibit limited relevance in securing human rights at the local level for those in need, such as asylum seekers and refugees, since they are mainly directed to the localization of the rights of the indigenous people. Notably, by seriously considering the human rights invocation of local actors (Oomen 2014; Baumgärtel and Oomen 2019) and translating their narratives into legal vocabulary (Frankenberg 2014), it becomes evident that each narrative is aligned with distinct theoretical frameworks and corresponds to specific legal rights. For instance, conservatism is associated with the right to property (Article 1 of Protocol No. 1 of the ECHR), while communitarianism intersects with the right to private and family life (Article 8 of the ECHR), which is also intertwined with conservatism. Global liberalism is manifested in the right to personal freedom and security (Article 5 of the ECHR) and additionally, in the prohibition of expulsion or return ('refoulement'), which is anchored in Article 33 of the 1951 Refugee Convention. Egalitarianism, on the other hand, is reflected in the right to education, particularly concerning minors residing at RICs (Article 5 of the ECHR). Narratives articulated by local actors categorized under impartiality emerge as influential resources for the glocalization of the human rights of asylum seekers and refugees. These particular local actors, capable of being identified as a type of significant human rights theorists, warrant careful consideration of their proposals.

10 Partiality

Communitarianism and conservatism

The foundational principle of 'partialism' posits that in policy formulation, the rights and interests of community members should take precedence over those of nonmembers. Proponents of this perspective argue that the influx of a substantial number of refugees into a society poses a threat to its cultural integrity, contending that refugees may inevitably bring about alterations in the political fabric and institutional structures of the host communities, including language dynamics (Gibney 2004, p. 29). The theoretical framework of 'partiality' encompasses political theories such as communitarianism, conservatism and constitutionalism. These currents diverge in their interpretations of various values; nonetheless, they concur that refugee policies are considered 'legitimate' when they align with the values and interests of the local society set to receive them. Moral primacy is accorded to the citizens of each society, as they are deemed the sole arbiters empowered to determine who may gain admittance to their respective territories (Gibney 2004, pp. 32–33).

The delegation of decision-making authority to members of a society concerning the admission of nonmembers is aimed at safeguarding the collective culture and identity of the community, while prioritizing empathy and care for compatriots remains paramount. Among the arguments advanced by community members, particular emphasis is placed on the economic ramifications of population movements (Gibney 2004; Boswell 2005; Turner and Fozdar 2010; Mantel 2019). According to this perspective, immigration policies advocating for open borders may potentially undermine the welfare state, impacting essential services such as healthcare, pensions and social welfare benefits (Carens 2013, pp. 88–109, pp. 225–254; for insights into the connection between immigration and the obligation to provide free medical care arising from individual rights, as well as the European Court of Human Rights' interpretation of Articles 3 and 8 of the European Convention on Human Rights (ECHR) regarding nondeportation of aliens on health grounds, refer to Kolliniati 2019, pp. 167–190, pp. 213–221).

Communitarianism

Communitarianism posits that the community assumes a pivotal role in shaping values, principles and institutions, as well as common practices. Within this paradigm,

DOI: 10.4324/9781003468134-15

'citizens' are delineated from nonmembers by their collective consciousness and shared 'common meanings', which emanate from a shared cultural heritage, linguistic cohesion and historical narrative (Walzer 1983, p. 28; Haus 2018), akin to the tenets of conservatism. Communitarian ideology asserts that the community holds inherent responsibilities toward its members, which are deeply rooted in their shared cultural identity and constitute an intrinsic aspect of their persona (Gibney 2004, p. 25). Critiquing liberal theories of justice, communitarians contend that the formulation of a universal theory of global justice is unattainable (Sandel 1984; Sandel 1998; Taylor 2001; MacIntyre 2007). Instead, they argue that principles of justice are intricately tied to each individual community and its 'thick' political values. Individuals are inherently tied to the communities to which they belong and their values and choices are profoundly influenced by the principles espoused by each community. Therefore, unlike liberalism which extols the primacy of the individual and emphasizes personal freedom and equality, communitarianism posits that individual choice cannot be viewed as autonomous. Rather, it is perpetually influenced by the collective identity and norms of the community to which the individual belongs. While contemporary theorists of political philosophy do not outright dismiss the notion of community, their scholarly endeavors have not prioritized the ideal of community (Kymlicka 2002, p. 208). Notable figures within communitarian thought include Daniel A. Bell, Alasdair McIntyre, David Miller, Michael Sandel, Charles Taylor and Michael Walzer.

Narratives that delineate distinctions between 'native' and 'immigrant' populations, emphasizing the numerical ratio between these demographic groups, align with the communitarian paradigm. Such narratives often employ specific percentages to bolster arguments regarding the causal linkages between the disparities in native-immigrant population proportions and the concomitant challenges encountered by the community.

> The RIC functions as an identification center, yet prolonged confinement due to enforced geographical restrictions can lead to quasi-permanent residency. Consequently, significant shifts in the native-immigrant population ratio pose challenges, particularly on arid islands. While minor population increases of 1% or 2% are manageable, during migration crises, flow surges, often dictated by neighboring countries, can escalate by 10% to 15%. For instance, on Chios island, with a population of approximately 50,000, periods of immigrant and refugee influxes have seen numbers reach 7,500 to 8,000, accounting for 15% to 16% of the population, resulting in evident challenges. Additionally, the immigration management sector, encompassing catering services at the Center and legal support mechanisms for asylum seekers by NGOs, faces compounded challenges due to the escalating population.
>
> (25/02/21 P20)

> It's unsustainable for 20 thousand people to reside in Lesvos, where the population of Mytilini is now smaller than it was in Moria. Similarly, it's

> untenable for the population of the RIC in Samos to surpass that of the city, as it did at one point. Governments must take responsibility to prevent such occurrences. There needs to be a comprehensive plan not just for reception, but also for integration. This includes assessing capacity and setting conditions for accommodating refugees. Currently, only the 'Helios' program addresses the integration of recognized refugees.
>
> (26/01/21 P17)

The concepts of 'our young people' and 'our young population' epitomize communitarian tenets, intimately intertwined with a particular community, notably the island, thereby accentuating the notion of belonging to a collective with shared values. Within this discourse, in harmony with communitarian precepts, the community assumes obligations toward 'its young population', stemming from their collective commitment to a shared cultural legacy. Moreover, communitarian characteristics manifest in the delineation between heterogeneous populations adhering to divergent principles. The narrative underscores the potential complexities arising from the adoption of disparate values by discrete communities. While the island community has cohered to the embrace of European values, the immigrant populace adheres to moral and cultural norms distinct from those prevalent in European societies.

> Young people in our islands struggle to find jobs here, so they often leave after finishing school and don't come back. This means we're losing our own young people, while the population on our islands is getting older. Additionally, the presence of the RIC exacerbates internal tensions, as accommodating a population of 50,000 alongside an immigrant population numbering 6,000 to 7,000 can statistically lead to instances of delinquency and clashes stemming from cultural disparities.
>
> (25/02/21 P20)

The influx of immigrants to an area can disrupt the equilibrium between Indigenous residents and newcomers, leading to adverse repercussions across various domains of society.

> Economic dependence on immigration is on the negative side. [...] Seeing an economy, an entire society, e.g. its hotels have a very large occupancy consisting of security forces, consisting of employees of supranational organizations, of NGOs, etc., if one goes to such a place and sees this proportionality of population in relation to immigration ... there is no healthy economy. A healthy economy should prioritize sectors like agriculture, manufacturing and tourism to provide jobs for locals and prevent population aging.
>
> (25/02/21 P20)

In an actor's narrative, a discernible dichotomy arises between the constituents and outsiders of the community. Although the actor himself does not belong to the community, being an operative of an organization rendering aid to asylum seekers on the island of Lesvos, he underscores the primacy of the rights and concerns of Greek nationals, denoted as the 'constituents', over those of nonmembers. Within this narrative, palpable tensions emerge between the Indigenous populace of Lesvos and the volunteers, including members of nongovernmental organizations (NGOs) and international entities, who have taken up residence on the island and engaged in immigration-related endeavors. The local community often regards such individuals with a measure of suspicion, a sentiment the actor deems occasionally justified. Nevertheless, as per the narrative, it would be unwarranted to castigate the locals as inherently prejudiced, as they, too, grapple with profound challenges attributable to the presence of the Reception and Identification Centre (RIC) in the region.

> Conflicting interests and commonalities exist between the local community and asylum seekers. Both groups share the sentiment of not wanting to be here, enduring the challenging conditions. This sentiment is echoed not only by the asylum seekers and locals but also by the municipality and firefighters. Despite accusations in the media labeling locals as racist and unwelcoming toward immigrants, this portrayal is inaccurate. The local residents have endured this situation for five years and understandably feel overwhelmed and disappointed. NGO volunteers should refrain from accusing locals of racism. However, some volunteers may approach their stint with a casual attitude, viewing it as an opportunity for a temporary break or leisure. This behavior fosters suspicion among locals, who may perceive NGOs as merely seeking leisure opportunities. This tension is understandable given the circumstances. Ultimately, there is a shared desire among all parties for the situation to be addressed appropriately, with adequate resources and support, whether in mainland Greece, France, or elsewhere.
>
> (19/11/20 P3)

In the narratives articulated by local actors, a clear demarcation between community insiders and outsiders emerges, yet a consensus prevails among the island's Indigenous populace, professionals and asylum seekers alike: none harbor a desire for the establishment's presence on the island. Within this narrative framework, the unequivocal rejection of the facility's existence is underscored, with the exception being some political stakeholders, for whom the presence of the RIC remains a deliberate political prerogative.

> I believe there is certainly some tension present… It's evident that Greek locals, understandably, would rather not have such a structure on their islands… I think that by offering aid and assistance to those within the facilities, there may be a concern that we are inadvertently encouraging more arrivals to Lesvos. This, in a way, could be perceived as a conflict of interest. However, personally, I find it challenging to answer this question definitively because, when you consider people's sentiments, none of us truly wish for

> these RICs to exist, for a variety of reasons. Naturally, the people within the RIC are dissatisfied with their circumstances and similarly, the local Greek community is displeased with the presence of this structure on the island. Thus, in that sense, I believe there is no inherent conflict of interest, as I think everyone shares a desire to find a solution promptly. It is widely agreed upon that the ongoing presence of these structures on Lesvos is not the solution. When I mention 'no one', I am referring to the Greek locals, the residents of the RIC and the volunteers and professionals engaged in immigration matters on the island. I am excluding politicians from this discussion, as their decisions regarding the status quo are inherently political.
>
> (30-11-20 P5)

> Neither the locals nor the asylum seekers desire to remain here. Asylum seekers are averse to being congregated in this manner, while the locals are averse to hosting such a large number of refugees. […] The construction of a new Closed Controled Structure has left both locals and asylum seekers feeling abandoned.
>
> (22/12/20 P11)

In the narrative articulated by a local actor, the RIC structure and the surrounding community are portrayed as interconnected entities – any challenges within the RIC reverberate directly onto the island itself. The deplorable living conditions experienced by refugees within the RIC cannot be cordoned off from the broader local community, as the latter cannot remain indifferent or detached from the circumstances prevailing within its vicinity. Within this narrative, emphasis is placed on the imperative of providing free medical care within the RIC, while concurrently acknowledging the paramount importance of safeguarding the health of the residents of the local community. This narrative evinces communitarian undertones, as it delineates a clear demarcation between these two interdependent communities.

> Too many essential provisions are lacking, which should not lead to such egregious infringements upon the dignity of those confined within. The principal challenge within the RIC lies in the sense of entrapment experienced by its inhabitants, coupled with the uncertainty regarding their future. Moreover, the living conditions within the RIC compound are an affront to their dignity. It is imperative that they be liberated from the confines of the RIC and facilitated by the government to safely reach their intended destinations and reunite with their families. Despite a decline in arrivals for various reasons, the premises of the RICs still grapple with hygiene deficiencies and staffing shortages, particularly in medical and administrative personnel. Ensuring the health and well-being of refugees within these facilities is paramount, as it directly impacts the overall health of the surrounding area. These elements are interlinked; inadequate conditions within the RICs cannot be divorced from the well-being of the broader community.
>
> (22/01/21 P15)

In a narrative, the presence of the RIC on the island is depicted as leaving an indelible 'mark' on the local community. This narrative underscores the adverse repercussions of the RIC's existence on the island, highlighting the marginalization of the rights and interests of the local populace by the European Union. Additionally, there is a pervasive concern regarding the Aegean islands being instrumentalized by Europe to advance its own objectives, while concurrently failing to provide substantial assistance to local government.

> To address this issue, we need stronger policies that haven't been implemented yet. Greece, acting as the EU's entry gate, hasn't received structured support for its challenges. Funds go to NGOs, but local government lacks assistance. This cannot continue. My statements are not mere political rhetoric; they reflect a firsthand perspective informed by experience and observation. It is imperative that the islands do not devolve into mere holding grounds for the convenience of Northern Europe. The islands shouldn't become warehouses for Europe.
>
> (12/03/21 P24)

In certain narratives, a discernible dichotomy is drawn between the 'in-group' or 'members' of society and the 'out-group' or 'others'. Within the narrative of a local actor, community members are often referred to as 'their own people'.

> We helped because we thought that in this way we relieved the climate of tension there, but we also gave the possibility to the neighbors there to feel safer there, to our own people that is, but also to the local community not to be aware of issues that could create for it an insecurity of their own.
>
> (18/02/21 P18)

In analyzing the narratives of local actors related to communitarianism, these narratives underscore the centrality of the community in shaping values, principles and institutions, emphasizing shared cultural identity and collective responsibilities toward its members. The delineation between 'native' and 'immigrant' populations, particularly in relation to demographic ratios and their perceived impact on community cohesion, reflects communitarian ideals of collective consciousness and shared values. Moreover, the narratives reveal tensions and challenges arising from the presence of asylum seekers and the operation of RICs on islands such as Lesvos and Samos. The influx of immigrants disrupts the equilibrium of Indigenous communities, leading to strains on infrastructure, resources and social cohesion. The rejection of RICs by the local community underscores a shared desire for resolution, reflecting communitarian values of collective agency and solidarity in addressing communal challenges. Furthermore, the narratives highlight the complexities inherent in navigating the interaction between local communities, asylum seekers and broader frameworks of human rights and global governance. They underline the need for nuanced approaches that balance the rights and concerns of both host communities and asylum seekers while acknowledging the structural challenges posed by migration flows. Through these narratives, communitarian principles serve as a lens for understanding the intricate dynamics of migration, human rights and community resilience, advocating for solutions that prioritize the well-being and cohesion of the members of the community.

Conservatism

The inclination to uphold specific values, principles and a particular way of life stands as a central tenet of conservatism. Within this framework, conservative elements may permeate various political ideologies, including liberalism, socialism or communism (Honderich 2005, p. 6). Among these principles is traditionalism, which underscores reverence for established institutions and customs. Another core tenet, 'political skepticism', manifests as a reliance on empirical experience over theoretical frameworks. Additionally, conservatism views society as an organic entity, wherein collective identity is derived from its natural cohesion (Honderich 2005, pp. 7, 270–274). According to Scruton, a prominent conservative advocate, modern nation-states serve as moral anchors, uniting individuals through shared territory, language, history and culture (Politis 2021, pp. 11–30). When confronted with the choice between reform and change, conservatives typically favor reform, as articulated by Burke, who posited that fundamental aspects remain intact amidst reform, whereas change risks altering the sacred and enduring facets of society (Honderich 2005, p. 12). Fundamentality, in this context, denotes the sacrosanct pillars of a society, which conservatives assert must remain unchanged. Hence, the conservative ethos emphasizes safeguarding the hard-won achievements of civilization against encroaching forces of barbarism, deeming them susceptible and in need of vigilant protection (Politis 2021, pp. 11–30).

In the realm of social philosophy, conservatism encompasses two primary paradigms. Firstly, there is 'reactionary conservatism', as expounded by Robert Filmer and Joseph de Maistre during the 17th to 19th centuries. Secondly, there is 'matriopathic conservatism', championed by theorists like Burke and Scruton, which underscores the significance of national identity, collective consciousness and shared values derived from language, tradition, history and culture (Politis 2021, pp. 11–30). These shared meanings form a continuum that demands preservation. In Edmund Burke's seminal work, *Reflections on the Revolution in France* (1790), the foundational principles of conservatism find their articulation. (Honderich 2005, pp. 113, 114).

At a pragmatic level, the policies of the 'new right' governments of Margaret Thatcher in Great Britain and Ronald Reagan in the United States of America have been closely associated with the conservative trend. Within the various currents of the 'new right', often characterized as neoliberal, a paramount emphasis is placed on economic liberalization (Honderich 2005, pp. 113, 114). Robert Nozick stands as a seminal figure in modern philosophical expressions of conservatism (Honderich 2005, pp. 8–9). Central to Nozick's philosophical stance is the advocacy for a minimal state, wherein property rights and robust individual liberties are safeguarded, premised on the notion that taxation amounts to coerced labor (Nozick 1974, p. 169, cited in Cohen 1986). Consequently, the sanctity of individual property rights (Honderich 2005, p. 301) and the liberty of individuals and entities to acquire property are foundational tenets of conservatism (Honderich 2005, pp. 113–114). A key point of divergence between conservatives and the Nozickian perspective lies in their beliefs regarding natural rights and normative theories of rights. Conservatives contend that within society, positive law holds paramount significance, determining the institutional guarantees of rights (Honderich 2005, pp. 34, 35).

Therefore, in this book, a distinction is made between the conservative approach and the libertarian approach of Nozick as their difference in relation to natural rights is fundamental to the approach of this particular study. Also, according to the theoretical scheme of 'bias' and 'impartiality', the two currents have been categorized into opposite camps of moral thought. That is, while conservatism is in the 'bias' trend by laying the foundations for 'closed border' policies (Gibney 2004, p. 23), Nozick's libertarian approach could be placed in the 'impartial' camp by developing arguments in favor of 'open borders' (Wellman and Cole, pp. 79–92). For conservatives, the starting point of each individual does not play a role in their subsequent development. Using examples, they try to prove that one's success and failure do not necessarily depend on one's social and economic background. Consequently, in conservative thought, demands for a fair distribution of equal opportunities are rejected (Honderich 2005, pp. 226–227). In contrast to egalitarian arguments for a just society through the distribution of equal opportunities, conservatives support the idea of natural aristocracy (Honderich 2005, p. 211).

In conservatism thinking, individual aptitude, encompassing talents and predispositions, serves as the determinant factor dictating one's access to resources and amenities. The emphasis lies in curtailing the scope of the public sector and its services, while concurrently bolstering the private sector. This paradigm incentivizes individuals to cultivate their skills, thereby enabling them to procure private services through remuneration. Essentially, conservatism posits that prowess and talent dictate one's acquisition of property and consequently, access to commodities and services (Honderich 2005, pp. 120–121). Put differently, society is encouraged to prioritize the support of the gifted while affording lesser consideration to individuals grappling with physical or societal impediments. This ethos underscores the primacy of physical prowess over social status in determining individual welfare. Conservatives advocate for policies fostering competition and unfettered market dynamics, thereby fostering an environment conducive to the cultivation of innate talents. Conversely, they advocate for minimizing social policies aimed at supporting marginalized groups.

Based on the outlined parameters, conservatism embodies several fundamental components. First, there is a proclivity toward safeguarding values and principles, exemplified by traditionalism, which entails reverence for established institutions and customs. In this view, society serves as the bedrock for individual identity, perceived as an organic entity characterized by cohesion and continuity. Second, conservatism manifests a predisposition against radical changes, advocating instead for incremental reforms that uphold the integrity of existing structures. This stance aligns with a preference for individual ownership rights and the unfettered ability to acquire and manage property. Moreover, conservatives typically reject the notion of inherent or natural rights, placing greater emphasis on rights delineated and protected by institutional frameworks, notably positive law. Furthermore, within the conservative framework, primacy is accorded to the rights and interests of community members over those of nonnatives or outsiders. This underscores a commitment to preserving the cohesion and stability of the community. Finally, community membership is defined by adherence to the established principles and values of society, with foreigners perceived as potentially disruptive to societal identity. Indeed, the influx of outsiders may precipitate a transformation in societal identity, potentially diluting cherished values and eroding collective identity over time.

The actors aligned with conservative ideology, when addressing the challenges within the RIC, predominantly emphasize the infringement upon the 'rights of Indigenous inhabitants' and the vested interests of the local populace. Simultaneously, they express concerns regarding national sovereignty and the preservation of cultural homogeneity within society, perceiving these values as imperiled. Specifically, actors adhering to conservative principles prioritize certain issues. These include narratives focusing on national concerns and the perceived threats posed by RICs on a national basis. Moreover, they advocate for approaches explicitly favoring closed borders. For instance, some actors view improved border security as a potential solution to the challenges posed by the RIC (09/03/21 P22).

> The establishment of the RIC represents a lamentable chapter in our history, precipitating a national crisis for frontline islands situated on the border.
> (09/03/21 P22)

In the same category, there are narratives that emphasize the infringement upon the private property rights of the Indigenous populace. Under this approach, translating the approaches of the local actors based on the ECHR, it follows that in the narratives of the actors who are placed in the conservative approach, emphasis is placed on the violation of the right of Art. 1 Prot. No. 1 of the ECHR regarding the right to property and Article 8 of the ECHR regarding the protection of personal and family life.

Moreover, in alignment with conservative ideology, wherein individuals are expected to access goods and services through monetary means rather than relying on social support, certain narratives emphasize the economic burden placed on municipalities and the potential for revenue generation through return fees. These narratives suggest that, given the absence of official management authority at the local level over the RIC, municipalities may not feel morally obligated to extend their services to minority groups, thus justifying exceptions to fee regulations. It is highlighted that public resources are utilized by asylum seekers, placing strain on municipal infrastructure, despite the lack of explicit responsibilities assigned to municipalities concerning the RIC. Additionally, municipalities are tasked with waste collection from the outskirts of the facility, incurring costs without receiving compensatory fees from RIC residents for municipal services rendered.

> The only relevant responsibility of the municipality is solely the waste management outside the RIC area, nothing else. And this is of course a request, because the collection of waste is a cost, an additional cost for us, which we do not even reap.
>
> (18/02/21 P18)

> But those who live inside the RIC are not prisoners. They can go out, move around the city. People live normally in the city and then go to sleep in the RIC. Having 20,000 people using the services that the municipality provides in the city, you understand that the needs are increasing. In whatever period tomorrow we have 20,000 people visiting, the city will need more service tomorrow. That's why I say there is an additional charge. They are small, but stacked up they are big.
>
> (26/03/21 P25)

> Waste collection from central points to designated areas creates significant problems due to overpopulation and limited infrastructure. The island has been continuously burdened by this population influx for five years. Tens of thousands passing through have strained structures and caused environmental and health issues. The lack of effective state governance worsened the problem. Financial support began in 2020 to compensate for unpaid fees, but previous years lacked adequate services, resulting in resource and budget deficits. The support aims to replace fees per population unit.
>
> (12/03/21 P24)

> No municipal authority, including Leros, was officially assigned responsibility for managing the RIC. However, municipal authorities are obligated to handle waste collection, water provision and sewage networks, even for areas like the RIC. Despite lacking direct responsibility, mayors are expected to address issues arising from refugees and immigrants, as citizens turn to them for solutions. The citizen will not complain to the RIC commander, nor to the Minister, he will complain to the mayor. He will complain to the mayor, without, I repeat, without the mayor having any responsibility.
>
> (23/02/21 P19)

The municipality lacks the capacity to plan urban development programs due to the significant time commitment demanded by immigration issues, despite the municipality's institutional lack of jurisdiction over the RIC. This narrative aligns with conservatism insofar as it prioritizes development policies over social support obligations. The presence of minority groups on the island is perceived as a hindrance to the implementation of development programs.

> Administratively, the municipality of Mytilini faces increased bureaucratic burdens due to immigration-related tasks. This diverts focus and energy away from long-term development projects, leaving the municipality behind compared to others. Approximately 50 percent of the mayor's time is absorbed by immigration-related matters, hindering future planning and development efforts.
>
> (26/03/21 P25)

In narratives, local actors emphasize their opposition to changes in the economic activities of the island. They assert that immigration activities alter the island's character and detract from its economic vitality.

> The economic and social landscape is shifting on these islands, with a growing reliance on an informal immigrant economy, often operating outside the tax system. This, coupled with procurement practices of unaccountable NGOs, distorts the islands' real economy, hindering their development prospects. You understand that hiring a security guard or a border guard does nothing to help the islands' development prospects. The islands risk economic dependency on immigration, exacerbating existing social issues. Studies show the North Aegean Region, to which these islands belong, is among the poorest areas in Greece and Europe, with a significant decline in GDP and tourism following the influx of immigrants since 2015–2016.
>
> (25/02/21 P20)

Narratives portraying the local society's resistance to changes stemming from the establishment of the RIC on the island, highlighting the adverse effects on economic and social dynamics, align with conservative viewpoints. Conversely, some segments of the local society dissent from these conservative perspectives, asserting that the coexistence of the local community and refugees is harmonious and furthermore, has invigorated the island.

> Some residents believe that tourism has suffered since 2015–2016. However, there are also those who argue that tourism was already affected by the financial crisis. The town of Vathy has come alive because of the presence of NGOs, in the houses that are rented, in the focus because of the people who are here to help the refugee. As a resident of Vathy, what I notice is that the coexistence of the refugees with the local community is harmonious. Some conflicts have only existed between refugees within the RIC and this is due to overcrowding and being forced to live in inhumane and degrading conditions.
>
> (25/11/20 P4)

The preservation of a collective identity, culture and historical narrative, as advocated by conservatism, necessitates societies to remain insular, closed off to those lacking common attributes. Conservative theory perceives societal closure as imperative, as the influx of foreign elements poses the risk of diluting the shared identity of its members. Consequently, conservatives typically endorse the establishment of facilities catering to foreigners in remote locations, distanced from urban centers. A narrative relayed by a local actor underscores this preference, as the ideal scenario for the local community entails situating reception centers in isolated locales, colloquially referred to as 'in the middle of nowhere'. Initially, the community of Vathy, current site of the RIC in Samos, expressed support for plans to relocate the facility to a remote area distant from Vathy. However, widespread opposition arose within the community upon learning that the proposed RIC's capacity would far exceed initial estimates.

> Samos is the only island where the RIC is located inside the city. Initially, plans for a remote 'closed controlled center' were met with some local support for its isolation. However, surrounding village residents expressed opposition. Despite pre-election promises of a 1,500-person capacity center, plans revealed it would accommodate at least 5,000. This discrepancy led to protests, including occupation of the construction site entrance to halt progress.
>
> (25/11/20 P4)

The narrative elucidates the adverse ramifications stemming from the absence of initiatives facilitating interaction between the local populace and asylum seekers cohabiting within their vicinity. From a conservative standpoint, the presence of the RIC on the island underscores societal divisions exacerbated by the dearth of antidiscriminatory measures at the local level. Despite cohabitation within the same spatial domain, the two cohorts remain segregated, fostering a heightened sense of conservatism toward the 'other'. The failure to implement strategies to mitigate the abrupt emergence of the RIC exacerbates societal tensions. For instance, the burgeoning population has strained essential services, resulting in diminished efficacy of vital institutions such as hospitals, law enforcement agencies and legal authorities. Consequently, animosity toward immigration stakeholders proliferates within society, cultivating an environment conducive to violence targeting asylum seekers as scapegoats for prevailing societal challenges.

> The unique aspect of Samos is the proximity of the RIC to the city, allowing asylum seekers easier access to goods and services, mitigating social isolation. However, there's insufficient state support for local infrastructure and public services. For example, the hospital was already understaffed. The city's population increase necessitates corresponding staffing and resources. Efforts to integrate the local community with immigrants/refugees are lacking, leading to xenophobia and racism. Incidents of violence against NGOs have occurred, potentially fueled by social media pages promoting hatred and violence against refugees and NGOs.
>
> (25/11/20 P4)

A narrative contending that the presence of the island's structure is eroding societal cohesion has elements of the conservative theory. Central to conservative advocacy is the preservation of society's core principles and values, encapsulating its 'common meanings'. Consequently, fostering cohesion becomes imperative to uphold the shared traditions intrinsic to the locale, prioritizing the welfare of marginalized islanders over asylum seekers in need. For the local actor, safeguarding the rights and interests of the island's inhabitants emerges as the paramount challenge.

> The social aspect is crucial, as residents have endured five years of poor conditions and dramatic experiences. Research shows that hosting a large number of refugees/immigrants in a city creates cohesion problems, leading to inevitable frictions and incidents. This negative energy makes the situation unbearable for citizens, who seek social solidarity and support. Current focus is mainly on managing refugee problems. However, there are also citizens who face significant pressure and the municipality will have to find how to meet this challenge, which is very big.
>
> (26/03/21 P25)

The crux of conservative narratives delves into the intricate dynamics of the local economy, governance and the mitigation of societal tensions. Within these discourses, assistance rendered to the structure is not solely viewed through the lens of safeguarding the human rights of asylum seekers but rather as a strategic measure to avert inter-community discord and assuage local discontent. Such narratives prioritize the protection of the rights and prerogatives of the Indigenous populace, grounded not merely in humanitarian ethos but entwined with pragmatic considerations (Miellet 2013). Moreover, an overarching aim within these narratives is the fortification of the local economy, particularly through the prism of tourism.

> We have no involvement with the RIC apart from waste collection. Our actions prioritize 'good faith' cooperation and protecting the people of Cos, local economy and society of Cos. While cooperation with other agencies varies, our role is limited as main powers belong to the army and police. Recently, we were offered a role in creating food and drink shops within the RIC, but we declined, preferring not to support an all-inclusive approach.
>
> (18/02/21 P18)

> We've carefully balanced like tightrope walkers, ensuring that Cos isn't seen as a migrant destination while maintaining a sense of safety for locals. Despite past challenges, including financial turmoil and earthquakes, we aim to present Cos as a secure destination. Our goal is to successfully manage the immigration issue, as Cos has a reputation for safety and resilience, despite being impacted by external factors.
>
> (18/02/21 P18)

In narratives portraying the interventions of local authorities, a pragmatic approach emerges, primarily focusing on mitigating tensions by prioritizing the interests and rights of the Indigenous populace. The concept of 'local pragmatism' encapsulates the acknowledgment that neglecting to address issues amplifies their consequences (Poppelaars and Scholten 2008), as such inaction is perceived by the community as administrative 'negligence' and a 'lack of responsiveness' to municipal appeals (Sabchev 2021a, p. 12).

> Different regions and municipalities handle this issue differently and it's important to recognize that. Our approach in Pyly village is to prioritize good conditions at the RIC to avoid tensions or disputes that could negatively impact the local society and the broader community of Cos. We strive to provide assistance to improve conditions, even though it comes at a cost we don't directly benefit from. Despite our efforts, we maintain our objection to the existence of the RIC on Cos.
>
> (18/02/21 P18)

> All decisions are made by the EU or the Greek central government. The municipality takes no additional action to improve the situation unless it directly impacts locals. For instance, if RIC garbage blocks main roads used by locals or tourists, the municipality may conduct emergency clean-ups to address the issue. However, they consider areas outside the RIC as not their responsibility and refrain from action unless it affects local interests.
>
> (22/12/20 P11)

Additionally, narratives depicting the alteration of established societal norms often provoke insecurity within local communities. Conservative approaches, wary of potential threats to foundational principles and values integral to social cohesion, tend to resist such changes.

> On Leros, there had been a disproportionate quota between the island's population and immigrants. This created insecurity among the residents.
>
> (09/03/21 P22)

One of the main demands of the local actors who fall under the category of conservatism is better guarding the borders.

> Borders should be better guarded.
>
> (09/03/21 P22)

> One solution is better border guarding. The whole situation has created anxiety and fears.
>
> (12/03/21 P24)

The establishment of the RICs on the border islands is widely regarded as a significant encroachment upon national sovereignty. The peril posed by the RICs' presence in the Aegean islands is accentuated, owing to their geopolitical significance and strategic positioning vis-à-vis the nation's territorial integrity.

> We can all make mistakes. But these are dangerous mistakes: for national reasons. They are overloading the border with such a large number of immigrants. […] It is a national disaster for such front line islands on the border.
>
> (09/03/21 P22)

> We believe it's crucial to swiftly remove Cos from the 'migration map'. This isn't just about Cos; it's about all the islands, as they form the eastern front of our national sovereignty in the Aegean. We can't afford to be vulnerable during times of uncertainty, political tension, or expansionist agendas. We must oppose any such attempts against our lands. While these structures may temporarily accommodate people, they should remain at their current capacity of 816 plus 474 individuals.
>
> (18/02/21 P18)

In essence, narratives from local actors aligned with conservatism offer a comprehensive examination of the intricate dynamics surrounding migration, property rights and human rights within their communities. These narratives meticulously analyze the impact of migration on various aspects of local life, notably the economy, tourism sector and the preservation of private property rights. A key emphasis of these narratives is the prioritization of local economic interests and the maintenance of tourism viability, reflecting the conservative viewpoint. While acknowledging the importance of upholding human rights principles, particularly in the context of migration, conservative narratives tend to underscore the significance of safeguarding the local economy and tourism sector as paramount concerns. Moreover, these narratives shed light on the process of glocalisation of human rights norms, advocating for an approach that balances global principles with local realities. By contextualizing human rights within the framework of common culture, nationhood and the local economy, conservative discourses advocate for a measured approach that takes into account the unique circumstances of each island. In contributing to the ongoing discourse surrounding migration, human rights and global governance, conservative approaches highlight the importance of prioritizing the well-being and interests of the local community. While acknowledging the rights and concerns of asylum seekers, these narratives underscore the need to ensure that local economic interests and tourism viability are not overlooked in the pursuit of broader human rights objectives. Ultimately, narratives from local actors aligned with conservatism provide insights into the complex interplay between migration-related issues and local economic considerations.

11 Impartiality

Global liberalism and egalitarian liberalism

The prevailing assumption within theories categorized under 'impartiality' posits that individuals within a community hold equal claims in comparison to outsiders who enter said community. At an ethical level, states are construed as international actors, thereby necessitating equitable consideration of the interests of both 'natives' or citizens and 'aliens' or foreigners. Put differently, states are expected to maintain an 'impartial' stance concerning the demands of their citizens and non-citizens alike. Universal moral values and conditions, inherent to all human beings by virtue of their humanity, underpin this perspective. Within such frameworks, no prima facie arguments can be posited to justify differential obligations favoring members of a particular political community or nation (Gibney 2004, pp. 59–82). 'Impartiality' encompasses various theories including global liberalism, utilitarianism, egalitarianism and libertarianism, each offering distinct approaches to the issue by emphasizing different arguments and considerations.

Global liberalism centers its arguments primarily on the concept of rights. Michael Dummett (2001) posits that when individuals refuse to assist those at risk of injustice, such as those forced to flee their countries due to fear of persecution or violence, they effectively become complicit in that injustice (Michael Dummett 2001, p. 27). Dummett argues that those compelled to leave their homelands have a legitimate claim to refuge and failure to provide it not only amounts to cooperation with injustice but also entails a degree of responsibility for it (Michael Dummett 2001, p. 34). Justice, according to Dummett, necessitates that affluent countries 'open their doors' to those from less fortunate nations. Furthermore, Dummett asserts that a state's obligation extends beyond merely accepting refugees; it also entails treating them with dignity, both during the asylum application process and after they have been granted refugee status. In this regard, Dummett criticizes the use of detention centers as a deliberate tactic to deter further asylum applications and entry by foreigners (Michael Dummett 2001, pp. 38, 70).

Utilitarianism directs attention to the potential consequences of policies aimed at restricting refugee entry into a country (Gibney 2004, pp. 59–82). Conversely, egalitarianism posits a moral obligation to support refugees, seeking to rectify inequalities stemming from circumstances beyond their control, such as being born in countries prone to generating refugees. Under this framework, citizens of affluent nations bear a responsibility to advocate for immigrants/refugees to

DOI: 10.4324/9781003468134-16

achieve global egalitarian justice. Libertarian thought, on the other hand, argues that policies limiting population movement across borders infringe upon individual liberty. In cases of conflicting rights – such as between individual and state rights – the primacy of individual freedom should be upheld (Wellman and Cole 2011, pp. 93–116).

However, despite the advocacy for open borders and the call for equal treatment of citizens and immigrants/refugees, the 'impartiality' approach does not assert that states bear an unlimited obligation to accept foreigners. For instance, according to Ann Dummett (1992), rights-focused perspectives such as global liberalism acknowledge that certain restrictions on entry into a country are justifiable if an influx of foreigners would jeopardize public order, national security or liberal institutions that require protection. Carens (1992a) contends that states with cultural homogeneity, such as Japan, may legitimately impose entry restrictions to preserve their collective culture (Gibney 2004, pp. 63–64). Moreover, according to Michael Dummett (2001), restrictions on foreign entry may be warranted, provided they are not racially discriminatory. The presence of individuals of a different race from the majority does not inherently threaten the cultural integrity of the natives (Dummett 2001, pp. 60–61). Countries with a right to restrict foreign entry are those facing issues of population density and overpopulation (Dummett 2001, p. 63), while groups that may be barred from entry include those posing significant risks, such as terrorists and criminals (Dummett 2001, p. 74). From a utilitarian standpoint, some restrictions on foreign entry are deemed legitimate when the costs to the state outweigh the benefits of admitting the individual concerned (Gibney 2004, pp. 63–64).

In the forthcoming chapters, an examination of the foundational tenets characterizing two distinct currents, namely global liberalism and egalitarian liberalism, pertaining to the notion of 'impartiality' shall ensue. Subsequently, an endeavor shall be made to assimilate within the respective theoretical framework the narratives proffered by local actors concerning Reception and Identification Centers (RICs), delineating their narration through the prism of metaphors, myths and arguments articulated within their discourses.

Global liberalism

For proponents of global liberalism, such as Joseph Carens (1992a, 1992b), Ann Dummett (1992) and Michael Dummett (2001), restrictions on the entry of immigrants and refugees represent a direct infringement upon the principle of individual freedom. According to this perspective, the authority of each community to shape its entry policies is constrained by the universal tenets of liberalism (Gibney 2004, p. 60). A prominent advocate of global liberalism, Carens (2013) argues that moral principles can be elucidated through empirical examples rather than solely relying on theory (Carens 2013, p. 194). In this context, the narratives emerging from RICs in the Aegean islands serve as a valuable resource for establishing moral principles. Carens draws upon elements of John Rawls's theory to support his arguments, although he does not limit himself to Rawlsian principles. He employs certain aspects of Rawls's framework to address immigration issues, an area that has received comparatively little attention in Rawlsian justice theory (Carens 2013, p. 298).

According to his approach, individuals' right to freely move and settle in different countries can be inferred from Rawls's work. Carens (1992a) contends that freedom of movement is integral to individuals' life plans, even in a hypothetical world where political and economic security are evenly distributed among states (Gibney 2004, pp. 60–61). Rawls (2002) refers to political communities as 'peoples', not states. In Rawlsian idealized 'realistic utopia', immigration issues would be eliminated as the underlying causes of forced migration, such as political, religious and ethnic persecution, as well as hunger and oppression of women, would cease to exist. However, Rawlsian theory does not necessarily advocate for open borders, as different communities may adopt divergent political principles (Wolff 1977; Rawls 1999, pp. 8–9; Talisse 2000; Carens 2013, p. 268). Rawls addresses the challenge of establishing norms to govern international affairs amidst cultural and political diversity. He recognizes that pluralism among societies is inherent to international politics, akin to the diversity among individuals in free societies. While not all societies adhere to liberal standards of social justice, Rawls envisions the possibility of nonliberal societies meeting certain criteria of decency, rendering them acceptable to liberal societies as equal participants in the global community. Central to Rawls' framework is the principle of toleration, which dictates that liberal societies refrain from imposing their values on nonliberal counterparts that meet a moral threshold. This vision of a harmonious world relies on fostering cooperation among reasonable peoples in the face of international pluralism, aiming for peaceful coexistence. Rawls proposes the 'law of peoples' as a solution, comprising eight principles. Namely, respect for the freedom and independence of all peoples, commitment to upholding human rights, adherence to treaties and agreements, recognition of the equality of peoples as parties to agreements, acceptance of the right to self-defense, prohibition of instigating war for reasons other than self-defense, observance of a duty of nonintervention, adherence to specified restrictions in the conduct of war. Finally, one of the principles refers to the obligation to assist people living under unfavorable conditions in achieving a just or decent political and social regime (Rawls 2002, pp. 35–43). Moreover, while Rawls (1999) acknowledges that immigration could be restricted to safeguard cultural and constitutional principles, Carens (2013) argues that this argument could reinforce Walzer's communitarian perspective on immigration (Rawls 1999, p. 39, in Carens 2013, reference 22, p. 337). Nonetheless, Carens (2013) incorporates elements of Rawlsian approach, such as the 'original position' and the 'veil of ignorance', to advocate for open borders and the equal value of rights for both citizens and immigrants/refugees.

Carens (2013) identifies three primary factors that give rise to pro-refugee obligations and inform why democratic states should generally accept refugees. These factors include the 'causal connection', 'humanitarian concern' and 'normative conditions' within the system that gave rise to modern states (Carens 2013, p. 195). The 'causal connection' engenders moral obligations and pertains to the states' varying degrees of contribution to refugees feeling unsafe in their home countries, thereby compelling them to flee. As an illustration, environmental refugees are referenced, highlighting that affluent nations bear responsibility for environmental disasters such as global warming and uncontrolled flooding. This aligns with the central idea of the Tragedy of the Commons, which describes a scenario where individuals exploiting a shared resource in their self-interest can result in its overuse, lack of investment and eventual reduction of resources (Hardin 1968). Consequently, due to this 'causal link', these states are morally obligated to send assistance or to open their borders in order to accommodate individuals who are compelled to leave their homes for such reasons (Wellman and Cole 2011, p. 106).

Accordingly, in the narratives put forth by local actors, emphasis is placed on the acknowledgment of a 'causal connection' between various phenomena, including wars and climate change. Within these narratives, there is a recognition of the interconnectedness of events and the responsibilities that stem from such connections. This acknowledgment extends to both the repercussions of armed conflicts and the impacts of climate change, highlighting the multifaceted nature of the challenges faced by communities.

> The solution lies in preventing people from being forcibly displaced from their homelands, whether due to war, political persecution, hunger, or climate change – a factor that is often overlooked. The key question is how to address the root causes of these crises. Instead of contributing to the problem by selling weapons or pursuing policies that lead to displacement, countries should focus on protecting vulnerable populations. This includes refraining from creating refugees through harmful policies. As a member of the EU, Greece also bears responsibility in this regard. Analogizing RICs to 'concentration camps', it becomes evident that such facilities are not the solution.
>
> (14/01/21 P12)

> Decisions regarding the RICs are beyond our control for several reasons. Firstly, they are intertwined with the root causes of why people leave their homes. Secondly, European asylum policies significantly influence these decisions. Since 2015, when EU borders were closed, an unfavorable climate has been created for the first receiving countries, exacerbated by countries like Hungary and Austria refusing to share the burden. Consequently, the islands of the Eastern Aegean have become de facto holding facilities for displaced individuals. The EU must intervene, showing solidarity with Greece. Additionally, Turkey's manipulation of refugee flows exacerbates the situation. The Aegean islands are now grappling with overpopulation and the confinement of asylum seekers. The overarching goal is to send a deterrent message to potential migrants on the other side.
>
> (08/03/21 P21)

> They probably don't want to give a solution so the question is whether someone who creates the problem, if they can give a solution to the problem.
>
> (22/01/21 P16)

In the category of the 'causal connection', we can also consider the narration that contextualizes the establishment of RICs within broader policies associated with the capitalist system, which often lead to specific conditions and policies resulting in wars. According to this narrative, organizations like the United Nations (UN) and the European Union (EU) bear responsibility for the wars that generate refugees, and consequently, they have an obligation to protect the rights and interests of refugees. The proposed solution is not to fund 'detention centers' but to ensure the safe movement of asylum seekers to their intended destinations. The narrative emphasizes the imperative of abolishing RICs in the Aegean islands, not for the benefit of local island societies, but to safeguard the well-being of refugees. In this context, asylum requests should be processed in countries like Turkey to halt the trafficking of individuals and prevent drownings in the Mediterranean. It is highlighted that the creation of refugees stems from wars and poverty. Indirectly accepting the presence of RICs on the islands implies indirect acceptance of policies that contribute to refugee creation by local communities (22/01/21 P15).

> Laiki Syspirosi's stance is that current policies, driven by capitalism, result in barbaric outcomes, including war, impoverishment and death. To address this, it's imperative to halt imperialist wars and competition for resources like oil and energy. Practical solutions should involve implementing proposals advocated in municipal, regional councils and labor movements. Specifically, closing Reception and Identification Centers (RICs), issuing travel documents and challenging treaties like Dublin can help. The UN and EU should shift from militarized approaches to facilitating asylum applications and safe passage to destination countries. This would disrupt human trafficking and prevent tragedies like Mediterranean drownings. Ultimately, the EU and member states must cease their interventionist policies to stem the refugee flow and respect individuals' choices to remain in their home countries.
>
> (22/01/21 P15)

The concept of 'humanitarian care' denotes a sense of moral obligation prevalent within societies to provide assistance to individuals in dire circumstances, a sentiment that may find its origins in either secular or religious ideologies ingrained within the fabric of each community. Within this thematic category, narratives emerge that center on the humanitarian crisis precipitated by the introduction of RICs on the islands and the subsequent complexities encountered therein. These narratives serve to underscore the evolving landscape of public opinion and the waning of humanitarian sentiments within local societies, particularly in response to the implementation of the EU–Turkey agreement and the imposition of 'geographic restrictions' (11/03/21 P23).

> On the island, the main challenge was the humanitarian one. The island suddenly found itself home to a second major city. In other words, the first city of the island that has 30,000 inhabitants and the second was the refugee city,

> either it was Moria, or it is now Mavrovouni. Thus, it is important to note that so many people came violently, they came suddenly, they did not come slowly to the island. This created a shock in the society of Mytilene municipality and in the island as a whole. At the beginning, the inhabitants of the island reacted in solidarity, reacted by putting humanitarian feelings first, supported this population in a unique way, in an impressive way, in a period of financial crisis, when people had no spare, they gave what they gave from their backlog. But this population [Greeks] got very tired and they got tired because suddenly the population grew too much.
>
> (11/03/21 P23)

The crisis within humanitarian principles becomes discernible through implicit indications found within the narratives articulated by local actors. Within these narratives, there is a notable reference to the escalating prevalence of racism within local communities. Moreover, another recurrent theme underscores the emergence of xenophobic attitudes, whereby victims of displacement and humanitarian crises are unfairly subjected to discriminatory treatment, rather than the perpetrators being held accountable. These nuanced portrayals encapsulate the multifaceted challenges encountered in preserving humanitarian values amidst societal dynamics marked by growing intolerance and prejudice.

> Let's combat xenophobia. Xenophobia is deliberately cultivated. The workers, the employees and residents of these islands are being poisoned, precisely so that they do not recognize the culprits of their own situation, but also the culprits who create the refugee flows and this is the biggest challenge for us to highlight the common culprit and fight together against the common culprit.
>
> (22/01/21 P16)

> The rights … not even the rights of the child are guaranteed, not even the rights of the refugees. Refugees are currently considered a hostile population. While the Geneva Convention describes it as a vulnerable population in need of protection. […] The way things are developing in the EU and with the political correlations that exist, the problem of dealing with the refugee problem in conditions of justice and rights is shaping up to be very ominous. This I think is an unpleasant prediction, but I think it is quite realistic.
>
> (11/03/21 P23)

The humanitarian crisis within the local community is evidenced by narratives that emphasize the strains induced by overpopulation and extended stays on the islands. These accounts underscore the dire conditions prevailing within RICs, reaching a climax with the September 2020 fire at the Moria RIC. Consequently, manifestations of local unrest have emerged, including protests, instances of xenophobia and racism targeting asylum seekers. Furthermore, there have been reports of attacks and harassment directed toward foreigners, as well as representatives and employees of nongovernmental organizations (NGOs) (26/01/21 P17).

> In the beginning, the majority of the residents showed their solidarity. But the climate has changed with all this overcrowding and nuisance that has been created, with the riots, the confrontations, the destruction of property, some theft phenomena and so there are citizens who do not want so many people on the islands. There are groups that may have conflicting interests because the situation is not easily manageable or not manageable at all.
>
> (26/01/21 P17)

> The immigrant/refugee issue directly impacted Cos society in 2015, with unacceptable attitudes from municipal authorities and the government. This fueled xenophobic and racist sentiments, deflecting blame onto victims rather than addressing root causes. The establishment of the RIC in the village in Pyli had negative effects on the residents of Pyli themselves because it is a facility that was set up quickly, that did not have the appropriate infrastructure. For example, even the drainage was missing, so it created a problem for the neighbors in the village. Thus, it brought negative effects to local residents, prompting some to express xenophobic views. Overall, there were failures in addressing the crisis, with responsibility placed on authorities and policies for creating and exacerbating the problems.
>
> (22/01/21 P15)

From the narratives of local actors, it emerges that the humanitarian dimension and the concept of solidarity can take on different dynamics. In this case, while in a narration there is a direct reference to the obligations to ensure the interests and rights of the refugees based on 'humanitarian concern', however, this humanitarianism refers to class terms and class characteristics of the refugees.

> We are trying to express this solidarity in a class-based and organized way, so that we feel in practice that we are class-brothers with the refugees. It is not generally and vaguely humanitarian this action from man to man, but it is from brother to brother. And at the same time we address all the people of Leros.
>
> (22/01/21 P16)

The third factor giving rise to moral obligations toward refugees pertains to the normative conditions of the system that underpins modern states. In essence, the contemporary system of state organization has delineated inhabited areas of the earth into sovereign states, conferring upon them the authority to control borders and regulate entry into their territories. However, disparities exist among sovereign states, with some exhibiting inefficiencies or inadequacies in governance. Consequently, a moral imperative arises for states collectively to aid those in need, thereby rectifying the injustices perpetuated by the shortcomings of the social institution known as 'sovereign states'. This underscores the necessity for states to exercise legitimate authority within a world characterized by fragmentation into discrete state entities (Carens 2013, pp. 195–196).

In addressing the question of obligations toward refugees, Carens argues that the foremost duty is to ensure their security and protect their fundamental rights. While refugee centers may serve as temporary measures, they are not adequate long-term solutions. Carens draws on the Geneva Refugee Convention of 1951, which asserts that refugees are entitled not only to physical security but also to the opportunity to become integrated members of society (Carens 2013, p. 203). Thus, fair treatment of refugees entails providing safety and safeguarding their basic rights. A prosperous democratic state should not segregate refugees from the broader community, nor confine them to camps that merely meet their basic needs while isolating them from societal integration. Over time, refugees should be granted the same rights as other members of society and be embraced as full-fledged members. This implies placing limits on the duration of temporary refugee status, allowing them the opportunity to belong to and contribute to their host community (Carens 2013, p. 204). Accordingly, local actors, as depicted in their narratives, underscore the critical necessity of ensuring that refugees are not subjected to extended periods of isolation from the broader society.

> We are striving to avoid the establishment of a large-scale camp where tens of thousands of refugees would be confined, isolated from the societal framework. Nonetheless, we acknowledge the necessity of a smaller-scale facility on the island. The uncertainty lies in how this situation will unfold; the challenge is whether our society can come to terms with the presence of refugees for the foreseeable future. Amidst periods of prosperity and downturns, it is imperative that we approach this issue with rationality. Failure to do so will perpetuate societal turmoil and tension.
>
> (11/03/21 P23)

> The EU-Turkey statement has significantly influenced the situation on the island, particularly through the establishment of 'hotspots' and the enforcement of geographic restrictions. According to this agreement, individuals seeking international protection are required to remain temporarily at the Reception and Identification Center until their asylum claims are registered, rather than until the entire asylum application process is completed, which, in some cases, can take years. Consequently, numerous families and individuals have been stranded on the islands, enduring dire living conditions for over three years. Tragically, incidents such as fires breaking out in camps, as seen in Samos, have left many people homeless. At times, this has led to thousands of individuals, including pregnant women and newborns, finding themselves without shelter or assistance on the streets of the city.
>
> (25/11/20 P4)

> It was in the current government's plans to create Closed Controlled Structures. But the EU does not finance them, because it does not consider it

> consistent with human rights standards to have completely closed detention centers and that is why they will not be done. In other words, in the end, the government's plans stumbled on European funding.
>
> (26/01/21 P17)

Within a narration, significant emphasis is placed on the enduring isolation of refugees from the broader societal fabric, resulting in their eventual ghettoization. This narrative underscores the adverse consequences associated with protracted separation from the social milieu, contributing to the marginalization of refugee populations. Furthermore, explicit reference is made to the legal entitlements afforded to refugees under international law, suggesting a nuanced consideration of their rights and protections within the broader discourse.

> They are attempting to construct sizable facilities on all the islands, as per the desires of the EU. Presently, the EU aims to erect expansive, modern structures on each island, equipped with all amenities, to accommodate incoming refugees. However, this prospect evokes images of sprawling refugee camps akin to those outside Lebanon, housing millions of refugees. Consequently, we adamantly oppose the establishment of such large-scale structures, which essentially resemble 'concentration camps', as they deviate from the intended purpose of Reception and Identification Centers to serve as long-term Hospitality Centers. Firstly, we object because this vision contradicts the future trajectory of the islands; it is unsustainable to accommodate such massive refugee camps on islands with populations of 100,000 residents. Secondly, refugees themselves express reluctance to reside in these centers. Thirdly, we oppose the creation of such centers as they would isolate refugees from society, effectively creating ghettos and depriving them of opportunities for social interaction, integration and education – rights guaranteed to refugee populations under international conventions. To address these concerns, we have convened a city council meeting to discuss the matter further.
>
> (11/03/21 P23)

As Carens argues that 'affluent democratic' states bear a responsibility to offer assistance to refugees, a corresponding narrative underscores the European Union's obligation to provide aid to refugees, emphasizing its status as one of the wealthiest entities globally. Within this narrative, there is a call for the distribution of refugees among EU member states, guided by a system of proportionality that considers each country's capabilities, including factors such as Gross Domestic Product, population size and unemployment rates. Furthermore, explicit and implicit references are made to the gross violation of the rights of individuals seeking international protection. Specifically, direct mention is made of the infringement upon the right to asylum, while indirect allusions point to Article 3 of the European Convention on Human Rights (ECHR), addressing issues such as human trafficking and proposing measures to establish safe passages and transit routes for refugees to mitigate the risks associated with illegal trafficking.

> The solution requires intergovernmental cooperation. Given that most asylum seekers originate from countries such as Syria, Afghanistan, Iraq, Palestine and Pakistan, the creation of 'hotspot' centers in countries like Turkey, Jordan and Lebanon is proposed. In these centers, pre-screening of applicants will be conducted based on the criteria of the Geneva Convention and the official guidelines of the UN High Commissioner for Refugees. Those from countries with high refugee profiles, such as Syria, Afghanistan, Iraq, Somalia and Eritrea, will receive Schengen visas and enter Europe. The distribution of applicants among European countries will be based on population, Gross Domestic Product and unemployment rates of each country. This way, Europe, as one of the wealthiest regions globally, could host three to four million asylum seekers in the coming years through proportional distribution. Establishing 'hotspots' in these countries would regulate human trafficking, prevent abuse and violence and provide legal and safe means of arrival in Europe, while simultaneously respecting the right to asylum as enshrined in the Charter of Fundamental Rights of the European Union.
>
> (26/01/21 P17)

From various actors, the unfavorable conditions in the RICs constitute a method of deterrence (Mann 2017) for refugee flows, while it has been reported that a lawsuit has been filed at the Office of the Prosecutor of the International Criminal Court against the EU for crimes against humanity.

> A lawsuit has been filed against the EU for crimes against humanity.
>
> (26/01/21 P17)

> It has been clearly stated that incentives should not be given to encourage [people to come to Europe] and that by creating such a situation. The refugee issue has been somehow instrumentalized, in Turkey's relationship with the EU and in Turkey's relationship with Greece, those people who have brought them to this situation, exploit them even more. Since they cannot reach an agreement with their partner Erdogan, they create such a situation [within the reception centers] so as to deter refugees from coming.
>
> (22/01/21 P16)

A narration underscores the imperative to safeguard the rights of refugees, while concurrently highlighting the contravention of the Geneva Convention through the application of the 'geographical limitation' policy. At its core, the narrative elucidates the formidable task of attaining equilibrium in the administration of refugee populations. Elements of global liberalism are discernible in the advocacy for upholding refugee rights delineated in international accords. Nevertheless, notwithstanding these endeavors, attention is drawn to the European Union's transgression of the Geneva Convention through the implementation of border closures, thereby presenting a substantial impediment to mitigating the refugee crisis.

> Striking a delicate balance is challenging; each place, every island and every community must strive for peaceful coexistence and work towards a brighter future. The equal distribution of the refugee population across Greece, which even the Central Union of Municipalities of Greece (KEDE) now accepts, is something we've been advocating for a long time. However, at the same time, we must uphold the rights of these people who are here according to international conventions. We mustn't forget that these people are refugees, with specific rights and there's a specific protocol according to which these individuals should be facilitated in their resettlement. However, the biggest problem arises from the fact that the EU is currently violating the Geneva Convention by closing its borders. That's where it all begins.
>
> (11/03/21 P23)

The narration highlights explicit references to violations of refugees' rights, emphasizing that local authorities lack decision-making power. However, they are noted to play a role in aligning with migration policies, even in cases where societal consensus may disagree with such alignment.

> At this moment, the EU continues to bear responsibility, as it is willing to allocate billions to prevent any refugee from crossing the borders of Greece, to keep them here and to create extremely luxurious concentration camps for us to detain the refugees who do not want to stay … and for the EU, this is a matter of human rights. […] The local level does not have a role, cannot make decisions at the local level. The local level can offer opinions. For example, the current local authority has a responsibility. In what sense? Because for political reasons, it aligns with the planning of Migration Policy and says Yes to the Center that the EU and the government want to establish. However, the entire society says no. Therefore, the current municipal authority is charged with this, in the sense that it agrees. Not that if it did not agree, the state could not agree directly. It could. But it is important to have all authorities with you.
>
> (11/03/21 P23)

In a narrative, human rights and the obligations derived from them are clearly delineated. However, governmental public policies play a crucial role in their implementation, either constraining or expanding their scope. Explicit reference is made in the narrative to the current period where human rights have limited application.

> Human rights have specific content, countries have undertaken specific obligations, there is international law, there is jurisprudence of international law, there are guidelines and practices of previous decades that constitute soft law in some cases. Therefore, the content is quite specific regarding the rights

> and obligations of member states to protect them, particularly with regard to asylum. However, government policies change regarding the implementation of conventions and obligations. It is the policy choices that change the more limited or broader application of human rights, depending on the period. We are now in a period of restriction.
>
> (26/01/21 P17)

The narration bears similarities to a global liberalism approach in that it advocates for not only the protection but also the provision of assistance and necessary resources for refugees to ensure their sense of security. Additionally, it emphasizes other fundamental rights, such as children's access to education. Elements of global liberalism are evident in the call for minor refugees to have access to education appropriate for their age, emphasizing that this access must be guaranteed and criticizing the longstanding deprivation of this fundamental right for many children.

> Every refugee population should not only be protected but facilitated and provided with whatever they need so that they can be safely resettled elsewhere. It is imperative to ensure them the sense of security. Additionally, the other rights mentioned include children's rights, such as access to education. It is crystal clear that every child should have access to education appropriate for their age and the opportunity to access education should be guaranteed. For many years now, hundreds of children have been unable to secure this right.
>
> (11/03/21 P23)

The challenges of providing education to refugee children and emphasizes the shared responsibility of both the state and civil society in meeting their needs, are discussed in different narratives. It also highlighted the mobilization of private initiatives, solidarity and community efforts to address gaps in education provision. Overall, narratives reflect elements of global liberalism in their advocacy for upholding refugee rights and the collective responsibility of society to support marginalized populations.

> Children have the right to education. So, whose obligation is it to provide education? At this moment, there are thousands … hundreds of children currently here, around 1500 children in the camp, but there are no schools. They do not attend schools and the reason is that they will not be permanently here; they will go somewhere else until their processes are completed. Of course, we used to have some children for several years, so for several years, they didn't go to school … so in this sense, certainly the responsibility falls on the Greek state. Furthermore, the conditions are often such that not all obligations can be fulfilled and this responsibility cannot be translated into specific actions. I think it is very good that here comes, we could say, private initiative, to fill these gaps. Here in Lesvos, there was an unprecedented

> mobilization of people, individuals, who responded to emergency situations to fill this gap. […] Fundamentally speaking, it could be said that it is the state's responsibility, but beyond that, I see that there is a collective responsibility of society, which fortunately many people, either individually or organized through organizations, mobilize to meet these needs.
>
> (13/11/20 P1)

In this context, narratives that explicitly reference violations of asylum seekers' rights, especially those affecting vulnerable groups, align with principles of global liberalism. This narrative underscores the plight of vulnerable individuals who lack support, exacerbated by instances of gender-based violence within the RIC, exposing survivors to the risk of re-traumatization.

> One of the main problems in Samos is the lack of suitable and secure accommodation facilities on the island. Until recently, there were some apartments under the ESTIA program that could accommodate about 200 to 250 people belonging to vulnerable groups. Now we have a huge population of vulnerable individuals who receive absolutely no support. Additionally, there are cases of gender-based violence within the Reception and Identification Center (RIC) and there are no accommodation shelters for survivors, who are forced to stay within the RIC alongside the perpetrators with the risk of re-traumatization.
>
> (25/11/20 P4)

> Law 4636/2019 was implemented as of January 1, 2020. Until the end of 2019, vulnerable individuals were referred to the regular procedure and could be transferred to the mainland to access more suitable reception conditions, as well as tertiary hospitals. The island has one hospital, the General Hospital of Samos, which is already understaffed, lacks all medical specialties, does not have medical equipment and is inadequate for the local population. Sometimes, the number of residents in the RIC had more than doubled the city's population. As of January 1, 2020, vulnerable individuals remain here (vulnerable groups e.g., pregnant women, women in labor, unaccompanied children, torture victims, gender-based violence victims, shipwreck victims, persons with disabilities, chronic health issues, etc.) and only some exceptional cases are provided for lifting the geographical restriction.
>
> (25/11/20 P4)

The narratives surrounding asylum seekers' human rights protection and violations and the safeguarding of minor refugees share striking parallels with key tenets of global liberalism. At their core, both emphasize the fundamental principles of equality, justice and human dignity. Global liberalism champions the idea of universal human rights, asserting that every individual, regardless of nationality or background, deserves basic rights and protections. Similarly, narratives concerning asylum seekers and refugees underscore the importance of upholding these rights, particularly for those fleeing persecution, conflict or grave human rights abuses. Moreover, both global liberalism and the narratives surrounding refugee protection emphasize the importance of international cooperation and solidarity. Just as liberalism promotes the idea of global interconnectedness and mutual respect among nations, narratives surrounding refugee rights advocate for collaborative efforts among countries to provide sanctuary and support for those in need.

Furthermore, the protection of minor refugees serves as a poignant reminder of the shared commitment to safeguarding the most vulnerable members of society. Just as liberalism places a strong emphasis on the protection of individual freedoms and the rights of minorities, narratives surrounding minor refugees underscore the imperative of ensuring that children, irrespective of their refugee status, are afforded the necessary care, protection and opportunities for a better future. In essence, the narratives surrounding asylum seekers' human rights violations, refugee human rights protection and minor refugees' protection resonate deeply with the core values of global liberalism, reinforcing the principles of universal rights, international cooperation and the protection of the most vulnerable.

Egalitarian liberalism

The concept of 'ecumenism' or 'universality' in liberal theories appears to lack practical application to the entirety of humanity. This assertion is substantiated not only by historical evidence but also by the observation that classical texts of liberal philosophy were composed during eras marked by colonialism and slavery (Wellman and Cole 2011, pp. 4–5). Nevertheless, despite the practical shortcomings of liberal theory, Cole (Wellman and Cole 2011) argues that the objective is to reinstate the application of the principle of 'ecumenism' and ethically defend 'impartialism'. He asserts that one's position on migration is pivotal to the coherence of the project of liberal social justice. Cole highlights that determining the 'just distribution of goods' and how 'liberal goods and resources' should be distributed more equitably is contingent upon establishing the 'membership status' within a society (Wellman and Cole 2011, p. 5). Who, then, should be considered 'members' of a society? In the framework of 'impartiality', the interests of both 'members' and 'nonmembers' of a society are deemed to hold equal ethical value. Cole (Wellman and Cole 22011) contends that border control policies should adhere to fundamental liberal principles. However, the existence of barriers preventing migrants and structures of immigration detention suggests that, in practice, 'liberal principles have been suspended' regarding border controls (Wellman and Cole 2011, p. 5).

Liberal theories, for the most part, have not systematically addressed issues related to immigration policy or matters concerning 'national identity'. Therefore, regarding the refugee issue, certain answers can be provided by examining whether liberal principles are satisfied (Wellman and Cole 2011, p. 2). According to Cole (2000), one of the challenges of liberal theory is the coherence of internal and external principles of liberalism. How will the principles determining the treatment of citizens of the state (internal principles) be consistent with those governing the treatment of nonmembers, i.e., immigrants (external principles)? For Cole (2000), the liberal dilemma is how these two sets of principles will be consistent with basic liberal values such as 'ethical equality of persons'. What he proposes to circumvent the dilemma is: (a) to accept that the role of the 'principle of ethical equality of persons' is relatively limited and can be bypassed by other particular principles, (b) to agree that the dilemma of these principles will be mitigated by using concepts central to liberal thought such as welfare, equality, order, etc., rather than invoking ideas of community or nation, (c) to understand that issues related to national identity are inherently 'nonliberal' or 'illiberal' concepts, making it rather difficult to achieve liberal coherence, although this simultaneously poses a problem from a liberal perspective. In this context, a liberal, egalitarian liberal, can defend strict immigration restrictions and claim that liberal principles apply only at the local level, not internationally. From this perspective, the ethical obligation of liberal states is to defend their own interests and those of their 'members', i.e. their citizens (Cole 2000, pp. 11–15).

The theory of liberalism constitutes a set of diverse principles and policies; however, some positions that could be characterized as traditionally liberal ideas include an emphasis on individual freedom, the promotion of a free market and property rights, the legitimization of politics and the promotion of a tolerant society. In the early 20th century, the concept of freedom and individual rights began to be questioned, giving rise to demands for promoting real opportunities for the socially vulnerable and reducing income inequalities. In the 1970s, John Rawls's work on the *Theory of Justice* significantly contributed to the development of egalitarian liberalism. Another prominent theorist of contemporary egalitarian liberalism is Ronald Dworkin, who distinguishes between 'option luck' and 'brute luck' (Knight 2005). Within egalitarianism, two prominent distinctions are drawn between 'luck egalitarianism' and 'relational egalitarianism'. Elizabeth Anderson (2010) argues that proponents of 'luck egalitarianism', including John Roemer, Erik Rakowski, Thomas Nagel, Ronald Dworkin, Gerald Allan Cohen, Richard Arneson and to some extent Philippe Van Parijs, emphasize the role of luck in determining distributive justice. Conversely, Anderson identifies herself with 'relational egalitarianism', aligning with thinkers such as John Rawls, Samuel Scheffer and Josh Cohen, who prioritize relational aspects of equality beyond mere luck considerations, claiming that equality pertains to the nature of interpersonal relationships since it necessitates that individuals perceive and interact with each other as equals (Anderson 1999, 2010; Voigt 2018).

Luck egalitarianism provides a foundational rationale for the significance of distributive equality. Certain liberals who adhere to luck egalitarianism contend that a distributive principle should address the impact of luck on an individual's well-being, as articulated by Arneson and to some extent, Cohen. Alternatively, others argue that the primary goal is to alleviate the influence of luck on the societal allocation of goods and resources among individuals, as advocated by Dworkin (Tan 2008, p. 665). Luck egalitarians assert that the objective of justice as equality is to minimize, to the greatest extent possible, the influence of unfortunate circumstances on individuals' lives when such circumstances are beyond their control and not a result of their own decisions (Lippert-Rasmussen 2001; Knight 2013). In an ideal luck egalitarian society, disparities in people's life prospects are absent unless they stem from voluntary decisions or misconduct, for which the responsible parties can be reasonably held accountable.

Elizabeth Anderson challenges the concept of luck egalitarianism and advocates for an alternative approach termed 'democratic equality' (Anderson 2010; Lippert-Rasmussen 2012). Within the 'democratic equality' framework, justice as equality necessitates the cessation of oppressive social connections. In an ideal society governed by democratic equality, the societal foundations of freedom for all are guaranteed, establishing a fundamental equality where each individual is in a relationship of equal significance, characterized by equal respect and everyone possesses genuine freedom to engage in democratic self-governance (Arneson 2000, p. 339). Nevertheless, Lippert-Rasmussen (2012) suggests that while her alternative vision of democratic equality is compelling, it still faces challenges. He argues that Anderson's criticisms to luck egalitarianism don't necessarily undermine its core principles. Instead, luck egalitarians can adopt Anderson's perspective, even on the topics where they may initially seem at odds, without abandoning their foundational beliefs. At most, Anderson's critique highlights the need to prioritize certain interpretations of luck egalitarianism over others, rather than completely dismissing the framework (Lippert-Rasmussen 2012).

In the context of egalitarianism considerations about individual responsibility are pivotal. In other words, luck egalitarianism tends to acknowledge and accommodate differences arising from individuals' choices and actions, while mitigating disparities that result from arbitrary factors or luck. However, according to Hurley (2005) while responsibility might help specify what to distribute, it cannot tell us how to distribute; thus, she argues, responsibility cannot tell us to distribute in an egalitarian pattern in particular. It can, however, play other important roles in a theory of justice, in relation to incentive-seeking behavior and well-being. In these terms, she proposes a bias-neutralizing approach to distributive justice in order to ameliorate the issues of responsibility (Hurley 2005).

The theoretical approaches that oppose egalitarian liberalism include the libertarian stream, as developed by Robert Nozick, the communitarian approach (see the previous chapter for the 'partiality' approach), represented by thinkers like Charles Taylor, Alasdair MacIntyre, Michael Walzer, Michael Sandel and theorists of feminist political philosophy (introduction of Paionidis in Dworkin 1992, pp. 20–22, 29–32). Within the framework of egalitarian liberalism, public policies should ensure equal rights, equal opportunities, equal freedoms and wealth for each individual, enabling everyone to achieve their life plans. According to egalitarian liberalism, the state should intervene, meaning it should favor certain individuals or groups, while rights can play a significant role (Dworkin 1978, 1984; Shapiro 2013). The goal of state intervention is to protect individuals from weaker social groups so that they can participate equally with other members of society who find themselves coincidentally in a more advantageous position. In egalitarian liberalism, the state is tasked with aiding individuals facing disadvantage due to 'brute luck', such as inherent social or biological inequalities, through targeted social policies. However, the state is not obligated to assist individuals who find themselves disadvantaged due to lifestyle choices, also known as 'optional luck'. This distinction is central to luck egalitarianism, which advocates for the state to prioritize assistance for individuals facing natural disadvantages stemming from biological or social conditions beyond personal control (Arneson 2000, p. 339).

Likewise, concerning refugees, these individuals are confronted with a disadvantaged status owing to arbitrary circumstances, specifically as a consequence of being born and brought up in states that are comparatively 'less privileged' than others. The situation they have ended up in, being compelled to flee their homes and seek asylum in other countries, is not a consequence of their own decisions or 'optional luck', but rather a result of 'brute luck'. Refugees, therefore, meet the criteria of 'luck egalitarianism'. In this context, adopting the approach of egalitarianism requires the development of public policies aimed at reducing inequalities between members of society and refugees who are less favored due to random circumstances. In line with the egalitarian principles of luck, these individuals deserve to receive assistance because the predicament they face is not a result of their own mistaken choices. Consistent with the principles of egalitarian liberalism, as per local actors, local government bodies should ensure the creation of better living conditions and safeguard the human rights of refugees.

> No one gets on a boat to leave their homeland, their family and face danger unless there is a reason for survival, whether it's war, political persecution, or hunger. So, it has to do with serious reasons for survival. We should protect them, they are desperate.
>
> (14/01/21 P13)

The narrative emphasizes the imperative of state intervention in safeguarding rights. Despite a marked disproportionality in the population ratio between asylum seekers and the local populace, the narrative accentuates the primacy of the state's obligation to furnish requisite support.

> There have been periods when the population composition was disproportionate, for example, five thousand locals to eight thousand refugees. Even individuals with good intentions feel uneasy because there is a lack of necessary support from state structures.
>
> (08/03/21 P21)

Simultaneously, the adverse conditions prevailing within RICs are attributed not to choices made by the centers themselves but to overarching decisions made at higher echelons of governance. The narrative posits that local authorities ideally ought to exert a positive influence. However, their capacity to effect change within RICs and advocate for the human rights of refugees is constrained by the hierarchical nature of decision-making, which manifests in conflicting interests.

> A conflict of interest arises between two primary concerns: the living conditions and human rights of refugees and the ostensibly humanitarian stance

> adopted by the EU. Paradoxically, the EU's central policy decision aims to render the lives of these individuals untenable to deter their migration. This decision not only compromises efforts toward alternative forms of governance, be they regional or municipal, but also underscores the complex interplay between humanitarian objectives and political imperatives.
>
> (14/01/21 P13)

Furthermore, as per the narrative provided by a local actor, the circumstances within RICs engender psychological distress among their inhabitants. This narrative not only critiques the policies and functioning of the RICs, positing that asylum seekers find themselves in adverse conditions through no fault of their own, but also implies that these conditions run counter to liberal principles.

> The term Reception and Identification Centers (RICs) serves as a euphemism for what are, in reality, akin to concentration camps. These facilities not only evoke anger among individuals but also frequently precipitate psychological issues, even for those initially arriving in good condition. Reports from certain NGOs shed light on undisclosed instances of mistreatment and exploitation within these centers.
>
> (14/01/21 P12)

A local actor explicitly invokes the notion of rights, employing the metaphor of 'double rights' and 'double solidarity'. Despite differentiating between the local population and refugees, this perspective diverges from communitarianism, as both asylum seekers' and local community members' rights are accorded equal value and deemed worthy of protection in the narrative. This narrative aligns with egalitarianism, wherein both members and nonmembers of the local society hold equal moral worth and there exists a moral imperative to extend assistance to those in need, considering the adverse repercussions witnessed within RICs affecting all involved.

> We advocate for a concept of dual solidarity and dual entitlement. A civilized, democratic society must confront the refugee crisis in alignment with the principles and values of humanitarianism, adhering to the tenets of international law while pursuing policies that guarantee both double rights and double solidarity. This entails safeguarding the rights of permanent residents – encompassing feelings of safety, unhindered access to public spaces and services, environmental cleanliness and smooth social and economic functioning – alongside upholding the human rights of refugees and guests, ensuring provisions for shelter, sustenance, personal hygiene, healthcare and education. Addressing the issue of refugee/immigrant overpopulation within our nation and on the islands requires concerted efforts on political, legal and moral fronts to foster solidarity, both from fellow European Union member states toward Greece and from mainland Greece toward the islands of the Eastern Aegean.
>
> (08/03/21 P21)

The narrative presented by local actors, emphasizing the imperative of ensuring children's rights to education and their seamless integration into society, resonates profoundly with egalitarian principles. Central to this perspective is the understanding that the state carries a substantive responsibility to provide free education to all children. However, as elucidated in the narrative, underage refugee children residing in Cos encounter significant impediments to accessing formal education. Even upon gaining entry to the 'Reception and Education Centers for Refugee Children' (ΔΥΕΠ) administered by the Ministry of Education, their participation is curtailed to a mere three to four months per annum. Furthermore, their integration into public schools alongside local children in Cos remains incomplete, as they are relegated to utilizing school facilities subsequent to the conclusion of regular classes.

> There should be care to ensure that refugee children have access to school classrooms.
>
> (08/03/21 P21)

> Refugee children in Cos attend school after Greek children have finished their classes and left the school building. They follow a separate program held from 2 to 6 p.m., which lacks integration into both social and educational contexts. In 2018, children registered in the 'Reception and Education Centers for Refugee Children' (ΔΥΕΠ) expressed dissatisfaction, feeling isolated in empty schools. Mediation and support services are essential, as many refugee children struggle to interact and integrate due to the stark contrast between their small group and the larger school environment. Thus, the integration of refugee children into schools is far from smooth.
>
> (22/12/20 P10)

When approaching the concept of community membership through the lens of a 'distribution issue', it becomes apparent that asylum seekers and refugees confront analogous challenges concerning the arbitrary distribution of resources and opportunities. This stems from the recognition that the designation of individuals as 'refugees' is often contingent upon historical circumstances beyond their control. Consequently, these individuals find themselves marginalized in terms of access to essential resources and educational opportunities. Specifically, underage refugees endure exclusion from a tranquil private and family life with abundant resources, a circumstance rooted in the historical contingency of their refugee status. This underscores the complex interplay between historical factors and contemporary socio-political dynamics in shaping the experiences of displaced populations.

Moreover, the incorporation of workers' rights considerations within the framework of egalitarian liberalism is feasible. Within the egalitarian paradigm, narratives emerge that underscore the instrumentalization of the refugee crisis and the establishment of RICs on islands as mechanisms to suppress workers' assertion of their labor rights. This narrative aligns with egalitarian principles by spotlighting the plight of marginalized segments of society, particularly refugee and asylum-seeking workers, who find themselves disadvantaged through circumstances beyond their control. It portrays RICs as instruments of intimidation and coercion against these workers.

> The Reception and Identification Center has indeed influenced tourism, albeit without significant financial impact on hoteliers. They have managed to navigate the challenges through various relief measures and subsidies provided by the government. One notable example is the reduction of the VAT rate, introduced not only as an incentive for locals but also as a means of coercion against the thousands of workers employed in tourism. This measure aims to deter them from demanding working conditions suitable for the modern era and higher wages, citing the pressure of low occupancy rates.
>
> (22/01/21 P15)

In conclusion, the narratives presented reflect elements of egalitarianism, illustrating the intrinsic relationship between egalitarian principles and the challenges encountered by marginalized populations, particularly refugees and asylum seekers. These narratives reveal systemic injustices perpetuated by the arbitrary allocation of resources and opportunities, as well as the exploitation of vulnerable groups within society. The focus on workers' rights further underscores the intersectionality of social issues, demonstrating how the refugee crisis and the operation of RICs on islands are utilized to suppress labor rights. By centering on the less privileged and emphasizing the disadvantaged position of refugee workers, these narratives align with the core principles of egalitarianism. They challenge prevailing power structures and advocate for a more equitable distribution of resources and opportunities, ultimately calling for greater solidarity and social justice within our communities. Moreover, these narratives indirectly highlight that by consistently upholding egalitarian principles, society can progress toward safeguarding the rights and dignity of all individuals, regardless of their background or status.

Part 5

Glocalisation of human rights

The last chapters of this book focus on the 'glocalization' and 'vernacularization' of human rights within the context of EU migration policies, particularly focusing on Greek islands. It explores how human rights norms are interpreted and implemented at the grassroots level, involving local actors such as mayors, councilors and activists. Despite global norms, challenges arise in translating human rights principles into municipal policies. The discussion covers EU migration policies and their implications, focusing on the use of procedural and physical deterrent measures to manage refugee flows. Specific tactics, such as the Dublin Convention and redefining borders, are employed to regulate asylum claims, often bypassing legal frameworks. This results in policies that may violate international standards, despite the formal existence of legal texts like the Geneva Convention. The narrative illustrates the tension between EU policies and human rights standards, emphasizing the plight of asylum seekers within the asylum centers on Greek islands. Despite legal provisions, states often fail to uphold international refugee and human rights laws, leading to a lack of solidarity and unified action in addressing forced displacement. However, amidst this crisis, local entities on Greek islands demonstrate solidarity through grassroots initiatives, showcasing the 'vernacularization' of human rights. The abstract underscores the importance of local solidarity efforts in upholding human rights and fostering solidarity with asylum seekers amidst challenging conditions in RICs.

This part of the book delves into the multifaceted dynamics surrounding human rights within the context of EU migration policy and its implementation on Greek islands. It begins by scrutinizing the 'externalization of EU migration policy', wherein the EU delegates migration management tasks to countries outside its borders through agreements like the EU-Turkey Statement and the Malta Declaration. Despite efforts to regulate migration flows, concerns persist regarding human rights violations in designated 'safe zones' like Turkey and Libya, exacerbated by legislative changes in Greece. The discussion then shifts to the contentious issue of 'pushbacks' at EU borders, particularly on Greek islands. This chapter explores the legality and implications of such actions, revealing instances of alleged pushbacks and the challenges in addressing them within legal frameworks. Human rights violations are a central concern, prompting calls for better compliance with legal standards and a more inclusive approach to human rights advocacy. Further exploration

DOI: 10.4324/9781003468134-17

delves into the complex interplay of human rights considerations within the migration discourse, highlighting both explicit advocacy for refugee rights by certain actors and indirect references to human rights violations within asylum centers. Efforts to address these issues emphasize solidarity and collaborative initiatives, while also shedding light on the impact of asylum centers on the rights of both asylum seekers and island inhabitants. Lastly, the concepts of 'glocalization' and 'vernacularized' human rights on Greek islands are examined, revealing how local actors interpret and implement human rights principles amidst the global refugee crisis. This chapter underscores the importance of international cooperation among municipal authorities and NGOs to effectively address refugee issues, while also addressing challenges within asylum centers and the diverse approaches to human rights advocacy within local communities.

12 Limiting the interpretation of human rights

The concept of the 'externalization of EU migration policy' pertains to strategies employed by the European Union (EU) to delegate political responsibilities or transfer burdens to countries beyond its borders (European Economic and Social Committee 2021). This policy approach involves utilizing instruments such as the EU–Turkey Statement (March 2016) and the Malta Declaration (February 2017) on EU–Libya cooperation, which delegate a portion of the management of migration and refugee crises to entities situated outside the geographical confines of the EU (Valenta et al. 2019). The hotspot approach is intricately linked to the 'externalization of the EU's migration policy' and the concept of 'safe zone' countries. Greece, in this context, serves as a pivotal 'buffer zone', aiming to regulate migration flows for the collective benefit of other member states (Del Sarto 2010, pp. 9–10; Valenta et al. 2019, pp. 164–167). In March 2016, the EU–Turkey Statement was enacted, with a primary objective to manage 'irregular' immigration and combat 'migrant/refugee trafficking' toward Europe. This policy aligns with the broader strategy of 'externalizing EU immigration policy' (Kotzur et al. 2020), utilizing Greece and Turkey as key 'buffer zones'. The agreement between Turkey and the EU prioritized intensified measures against migrant/refugee smugglers, coupled with the deployment of North Atlantic Treaty Organization forces in the Aegean region. As part of this accord, it was stipulated that 'irregular' immigrants crossing from Turkey to the Greek islands after 20 March 2016, would be returned to Turkey. Additionally, for each Syrian individual returned from the Greek islands to Turkey, another Syrian would be resettled within the EU.

The EU–Turkey Statement outlined provisions for the allocation of 3 billion euros from the EU to Turkey for the 'Facility for Refugees' in Turkey, with the commitment of additional funding of up to 3 billion euros by the end of 2018 upon the full utilization of these resources. Additionally, the Agreement stipulated that Turkey would facilitate the rapid return of all migrants not in need of international protection who entered Greece through its territory and would also accept the return of all 'irregular' migrants intercepted in Turkish waters (European Commission 2015b, 2015c; European Council 2016; European Parliament 2016). According to the narratives of local actors, the interpretation of the final clause is intertwined with the 'geographical restriction' of asylum seekers on the islands and the completion of the asylum procedure in the Aegean islands. Turkey's acceptance of

DOI: 10.4324/9781003468134-18

immigrant returns is contingent upon these conditions being met. This EU–Turkey Statement reflects the broader strategy of 'externalizing' the EU's migration policy.

The implicated actors encompass nations such as Turkey and Libya, which are designated as 'safe countries of entry' for individuals seeking international protection. Nevertheless, concerns regarding human rights violations persist within both of these nations. Numerous human rights organizations contest Turkey's status as a safe haven where asylum seekers and refugees can access adequate support. Reports from entities like Amnesty International and Human Rights Watch document instances where refugees, following periods of detention and mistreatment, are forcibly returned to Syria from Turkey under the guise of voluntary repatriation (Kyilah 2021). In response to these issues, a group of legal professionals has submitted a *Communication* to the International Criminal Court (ICC), alleging crimes against humanity by the EU. The Communication to the ICC (2019) targets the EU's migration policies in the Central Mediterranean and Libya between 2014 and 2019. It asserts that the EU and its highest-ranking officials from member states are culpable for crimes against humanity stemming from policies implemented since 2014, with the objective of curtailing migration flows via the Central Mediterranean route.

The border externalization strategies adopted by the EU, notably through agreements with Libya in 2014 and 2016, have had dire consequences, including the deaths of thousands of migrants and the refoulement of tens of thousands who sought to escape Libya. These policies have raised concerns about the EU's complicity in the atrocities occurring within Libyan detention centers. Crimes associated with these policies encompass deportation, persecution, murder, imprisonment, enslavement, torture and rape (Communication to the ICC 2019, p. 8). In the context of the 'externalization of EU policy', the application of human rights principles is significantly curtailed (Ciliberto 2021, pp. 204–205). Under the EU–Turkey Statement, individuals are deported to Turkey and subsequently repatriated to the very locations they fled to seek international protection. Consequently, this violates the principle of nonrefoulement enshrined in Article 33 of the 1951 Geneva Convention relating to the Status of Refugees. Moreover, this breach leads to a cascade of other rights violations, including the right to protection against inhuman and degrading treatment (Article 3 of the European Convention on Human Rights) and the right to a fair trial (Othman (Abu Qatada) v United Kingdom, No. 8139/09, 17 January 2012, par. 235–258). Additionally, the prohibition of collective deportations is rooted in Article 4 of Protocol No. 4 of the ECHR, which prohibits group refoulements and is further supported by the right to a fair and effective trial before national courts protected in Article 13 of the ECHR. According to the Communication to ICC (2019), between January 2014 and the end of July 2017, over 14,500 individuals either perished or went missing attempting to reach Europe by sea. Consequently, the EU's migration policy has transformed the Central Mediterranean into the world's deadliest migration route (Communication to the ICC 2019, p. 4).

The EU–Turkey Statement has been subject to criticism primarily due to provisions that allow asylum claims to be deemed 'inadmissible' under certain circumstances. According to Article 56 of the Greek Asylum Law 4375/2016 which was repealed in 2019 and Article 38 of Directive 2013/32/EU, if Turkey is categorized as a 'safe third country', asylum claims may be rejected. Similarly, under Article 55 of the Greek Asylum Law 4375/2016 which was abolished in 2019 and Article 35 of Directive 2013/32/EU, Turkey could be considered a 'first country of asylum', leading to similar outcomes. These provisions have sparked concerns regarding the adequacy of Turkey's asylum procedures and its capacity to provide genuine protection to asylum seekers, prompting questions about the fairness and effectiveness of the EU–Turkey Statement (Ziebritzki 2018, 2020). Furthermore, in Greece, the legislative framework established by Law 4636/2019 (subsequently amended by Law 4939/2022), effective from 1 January 2020, while not exclusively targeting vulnerable groups, manifests heightened challenges within the Reception and Identification Centers (RICs), impacting them. Prior to the conclusion of 2019, vulnerable groups were subject to processes affording the possibility of inland transfer and access to various facilities, including hospitals. However, following the enactment of this law, such avenues were no longer available to vulnerable categories of asylum seekers. The islands, grappling with a sole understaffed General Hospital, witnessed an increased burden on the health system. Since 1 January 2020, vulnerable groups, encompassing pregnant women, those on maternity leave, unaccompanied children, victims of torture, victims of gender-based violence, individuals with disabilities, chronic conditions, etc., continue to reside on the islands. The removal of the 'geographic restriction' is contemplated solely for specific exceptional cases within vulnerable groups. In essence, these legal changes have amplified the strain on the already stretched resources and services available to vulnerable asylum seekers, underscoring human rights and the complex and evolving landscape of refugee support systems in Greece.

In this context, the overarching policy framework that establishes RICs on the islands and constrains the interpretation of human rights is closely tied to EU policies. These policies not only shape the conditions within RICs but also influence the implementation of human rights standards. Despite efforts to integrate human rights into local policies, challenges persist, particularly in the glocalization of human rights discourse. EU policies often prioritize administrative concerns over human rights considerations, leading to a disconnect between international human rights norms and local practices. Furthermore, the legislative changes and their subsequent amendments, have exacerbated the challenges faced by vulnerable asylum seekers. The removal of avenues for inland transfer and access to essential services for vulnerable groups has placed additional strain on the already overstretched resources and services available in RICs. This has resulted in significant human rights violations, particularly for vulnerable populations such as pregnant women, unaccompanied children, victims of torture and individuals with disabilities or chronic conditions.

The EU's externalization policies, including agreements with countries like Turkey and Libya, have also contributed to the erosion of human rights protections for asylum seekers. The EU–Turkey Statement, for example, has been criticized for allowing asylum claims to be deemed 'inadmissible' and for failing to ensure adequate protection for asylum seekers in Turkey. In light of these challenges, it is evident that the glocalization of human rights in the context of RICs is hindered by a complex interplay of factors, including local interpretations, EU policies and legislative changes. Despite efforts to promote human rights, particularly from human rights supporters, the reality on the ground suggests that human rights are often compromised rather than upheld. As such, there is an urgent need for comprehensive reforms to ensure the protection of human rights for all asylum seekers, regardless of their location or legal status.

13 Pushbacks

Human rights organizations, both national and European, along with international bodies and civil society groups, consistently document cases of people apprehended after crossing borders irregularly and then removed without proper identification procedures (European Parliament 2021). The act of denying entry at a state's borders or orchestrating direct expulsions from its territory concerning individuals seeking international protection, absent prior scrutiny of asylum requests, is commonly termed 'pushbacks' (Council of Europe 2019; Ciliberto 2021, p. 204; European Parliament 2021). The discourse surrounding 'pushbacks' has been accentuated in the narratives concerning the asylum centers at the Greek islands put forth by local actors.

Refusals, whether they are carried out from the territory of a state or from its borders, are illegal as they are contrary to international and European law. In the event that a person has managed to enter the territory of a state and is deported without the prior examination of his request, this is a flagrant violation of the principle of nonrefoulement. But does the same apply to those who are at the borders of a state and have not managed to enter its territory? What about the rescues of those trying to reach the Aegean islands by boat in order to seek international protection? Do the local actors have the right and/or the obligation to rescue them, thus intervening in an area of competence of the Hellenic Coast Guard? As discussed in the third chapter of this book (refer to Chapter 3: 'EU and National Legal Provisions about Asylum Seekers'), the presented text essentially outlines the legal parameters governing the right to seek asylum at state borders and the provision of rescue assistance, primarily within the European Union (EU) and the Greek legislative context. First, Directive 2013/32/EU and Greek Law 4939/2022 establish the right to apply for asylum at borders, specifying procedures at the nation's ports or airports. Second, according to Law 4825/2021, both local and international entities possess the right to provide rescue aid within the jurisdiction of the Hellenic Coast Guard, contingent upon collaboration with duly registered Non-governmental Organisations. Compliance with legal provisions is paramount, requiring incorporation into emergency plans and the securing of written approval. Third, a legal obligation to provide assistance is mandated by the Criminal Code, with penalties for deliberate failure to rescue, highlighting the delicate balance between humanitarian considerations and legal constraints within the Greek legal framework.

DOI: 10.4324/9781003468134-19

In contravention of stipulations outlined in international, national and European legal frameworks, certain narratives conveyed by interviewed local actors suggest a departure from the observance of the nonrefoulement principle, manifesting in instances of refoulements or 'pushbacks'. Notably, in the presence of Frontex vessels in Samos, a local actor discerns that the term 'pushback' is employed under the guise of a 'rescue', despite reported instances of forceful pushbacks (03/08/21 P21). Allegations point to Greek authorities either repelling individuals into the sea before they can reach the island or, according to testimonies, apprehending those who have successfully arrived, asserting their intention to seek asylum, compelling them onto 'closed liferafts' and subsequently facilitating their return to Turkey (25/11/20 P4).

Within an alternative narrative, grievances surface concerning the occurrence of pushbacks. This particular account distinctly articulates allegations of transgressions against the right to seek asylum and violations of Article 3 of the European Convention on Human Rights (ECHR), encompassing safeguards against inhuman treatment and torture.

> Another pertinent concern revolves around informal deportations, eliciting grievances not only from foreign media outlets such as Der Spiegel and The Guardian but also through official statements from entities including the UN High Commissioner, the International Organization for Migration and the National Commission for Human Rights. These sources allude to credible complaints of deportations originating both from the islands and the Evros region, flagrantly infringing not only upon the right to seek asylum but also compromising the physical integrity of the affected foreign individuals.
>
> (26/01/21 P17)

> In my perspective, the establishment of the RIC does not represent a viable solution; rather, it contributes to an impasse. The implications of such a deadlock encompass issues of substandard living conditions, procedural delays in the asylum system and the execution of unlawful deportations. This strategy is not unique to Greece, as similar practices are observed in other nations. Examining broader Mediterranean policies, especially those involving Libya and Italy, reveals instances where rescue operations have been curtailed through agreements with Libyan authorities for repatriation. Consequently, it becomes evident that this approach aligns with a broader policy of deterrence.
>
> (26/01/21 P17)

The discourse highlights precarious circumstances, raising the prospect of pushbacks. The narrative underscores the expeditious handling of asylum applications, prompting inquiries into the mechanisms supporting prompt decisions and the government's prioritization of swift processing. The inherent precariousness of the situation is exacerbated by the dearth of transparency in the divulged conditions. Although direct access to individuals' asylum claims is elusive, substantial insights are gleaned from indirect information obtained directly from the asylum seekers themselves. A significant apprehension lies in the potential incidence of pushbacks encountered by asylum seekers.

> Concerns are voiced over the expedited processing of asylum applications, with questions arising about the mechanisms facilitating swift decisions and the government's emphasis on rapid processing. This uncertainty extends into 2021, particularly regarding the conclusion of the ESTIA housing program by ARSIS in December, contributing to the prevailing precariousness. The impending conclusion of the program leaves individuals in a state of flux, unsure of their future destinations. Key challenges involve the adequacy of asylum decision deliveries and the potential occurrence of pushbacks experienced by asylum seekers. The lack of transparency in disclosed conditions further underscores the overarching precarious nature of the situation. Information gathered indirectly through parents of children, as we lack direct access to individuals' asylum claims and do not engage in case management, adds to our understanding of the situation through the presence of our students on the island.
>
> (22/12/20 P10)

As asserted by a local actor, a profusion of complaints has been registered regarding instances of pushbacks to Turkey, albeit the validation of these claims proves exceptionally challenging.

> Numerous complaints have surfaced regarding pushbacks and notably, instances of pushbacks have been reported even from the Reception and Identification Centre (RIC). The practice entails transporting individuals from within the RIC and sending them away via boat. Interestingly, while not directly attributed to Frontex officially, concerns are raised about the organization's role in such incidents. This case, now communicated as information, has been publicly disclosed in the press, yet no formal investigation has been undertaken. Despite the presence of supporting evidence such as photos and videos, there seems to be a lack of official scrutiny. The absence of examination by an authoritative body makes it challenging for ordinary citizens or solidarity organizations to investigate independently due to associated costs involving legal proceedings. Nonetheless, the available information is duly reported … and at least we can just report them.
>
> (11/03/21 P23)

Research from various EU institutions, including the European Parliament (Dumbrava 2020; Radjenovic 2020, 2021), national and European human rights bodies, international organizations and civil society groups consistently document instances of pushbacks at EU borders. In response to concerns raised by the European Parliament, the European Union Agency for Fundamental Rights (FRA) issued a report in 2020 focusing on fundamental rights compliance at the EU's external borders, offering recommendations for better implementation of relevant EU laws. Additionally, the Parliamentary Assembly of the Council of Europe expressed alarm over pushback actions by EU Member States in 2019, citing violations of asylum seekers' and refugees' rights. Both the United Nations High Commissioner for Refugees (UNHCR) and the International Organization for Migration (IOM) have urged the EU and its Member States to cease pushbacks, collective expulsions and violence against migrants and refugees. A 2020 report by Refugee Rights Europe and the End Pushbacks Partnership provides further detail on pushback practices and associated border violence, highlighting their adverse effects on individuals' lives and European social cohesion (Council of Europe 2019; European Union Agency for Fundamental Rights 2020; European Parliament 2021; UNHCR 2021a; UNHCR 2021b).

In June 2020, the Greek Ombudsman, Andreas Pottakis, articulated concerns about pushbacks in the annual Ombudsman report presented to the Committee on Institutions and Transparency of the Parliament. The grievances centered around the perceived inadequacy of ensuring the independence of Frontex observers, coupled with a lack of transparency and accountability concerning Frontex's management of 'forced returns of irregular immigrants'. The complaint specifically raised reservations regarding the autonomy and accountability of Frontex's EU Pool of Monitors assigned to European forced return operations. Furthermore, the June 2020 annual report documented three complaints against Frontex for alleged rights violations related to pushbacks to Turkey (see Ombudsman, Annual Report 2020, p. 135). Approximately a year subsequent to the research interviews and two years post the Ombudsman's complaint, on 7 April 2022, the Council of Europe issued denunciations regarding pushbacks at the territorial and maritime borders of Europe. The Council of Europe emphasized the alarming normalization of pushbacks, characterizing it as a concerning trend. Commissioner Dunja Mijatović from the Council of Europe urged governments and parliamentarians to take decisive action to halt these practices, emphasizing the imperative of protecting human rights in Europe (Council of Europe 2022; Rankin 2022).

Solidarity actors and organizations meticulously document consequential human rights transgressions inherent in instances of pushbacks. This discerning scrutiny serves to underscore the intrinsic connection between pushbacks, which, by definition, imply violations of human rights. Subsequently, these local actors catalyze an assiduous pursuit of justice, articulating a nuanced narrative that illuminates the intricacies of such violations within the broader local context. From this vantage point, it is evident that the paradigm of human rights has traversed to the diminutive Greek islands. The defense and explication of human rights transpire through the agency of local actors, discerning instances of human rights transgressions resulting from pushbacks within a localized milieu, thereby instigating a pursuit of justice and rectitude. In this trajectory, the phenomenon of vernacularization and glocalisation of human rights (Merry 2006; Goodale 2007; Levitt and Merry 2009; Merry and Levitt 2017) manifests itself on the Greek islands. It entails the extraction and transmutation of ideas and practices originating from the global ambit of international treaties and human rights organizations, undergoing a translation process that aligns them with the inherent values and modi operandi of local contexts (Merry and Levitt 2017, p. 213). This transformative process is orchestrated through the nuanced comprehension of local actors who, in solidarity with asylum seekers, contribute to the assimilation of these ideas into the indigenous socio-cultural tapestry. However, their ability to actively advocate for asylum seekers' rights is constrained to reporting these violations related to pushbacks. Furthermore, the implementation of 'forced returns of irregular immigrants', colloquially known as 'pushbacks', underscores a profound erosion, rather than an enhancement, of human rights at the local level.

The inadequacy of human rights in providing effective protection for individuals in dire circumstances becomes conspicuous within this contextual framework. Derived from the narratives articulated by local actors, a salient determinant surfaces concerning the preservation of the rule of law and the realization of human rights: legal processes are inherently interwoven with financial limitations. The financial constraints encountered by these entities impede their capacity to engage in legal recourse to assert human rights safeguards. In the practical milieu, the integrity of human rights finds itself drowned in the Aegean Sea during the occurrence of pushbacks within the confines of the Aegean islands. Mark Goodale (2022) endorses a paradigm shift toward reimagining human rights, underscored by a critical reassessment of human rights institutionalism and political theory. This proposed transformation advocates prioritizing the 'practice of human rights' over prevailing practice-dependent theories. Goodale introduces the ethical concept of 'translocality', challenging the presupposed universality of human rights. Instead, it posits the cultivation of alliances supporting collective action beyond conventional boundaries of community, nation or religion. The envisaged paradigm shift necessitates a concerted endeavor to address global challenges, urging a departure from the conventional universality of human rights in favor of embracing 'translocality' and facilitating the expeditious formation of novel alliances transcending established dichotomies (Goodale 2022, pp. 7–8).

Notwithstanding the observable collective actions of local actors that surmount religious, national, political or other differentiations, the actualization of human rights appears elusive in practice. While the overarching objective, as posited by Goodale (2022), involves transcending global challenges to realize human rights, a pressing inquiry persists. In the current milieu, wherein individuals seeking international protection face the ordeal of pushbacks, a conspicuous imperative emerges. Given the protracted nature of global challenges, such as ongoing conflicts, a critical inquiry arises: what current initiatives are being pursued and of greater significance, what proactive measures should have been instituted expeditiously to safeguard human rights at the grassroots level? In the pursuit of actualizing human rights locally, unfettered access to legal instruments becomes paramount for local actors. While actions of solidarity possess inherent merit, their efficacy alone proves inadequate. Financial impediments must be dismantled to provide actors with the practical opportunities required to advocate for and safeguard the glocalization of human rights.

14 Portraying the relationship between human rights and Reception and Identification Centers (RICs) in Chios, Cos, Leros, Lesvos, Samos

The focal issues articulated by the diverse actors in their discourse shed light on the pivotal role attributed to human rights within their narratives. To examine the significance of human rights within the narratives elucidated by the interviewees in this study, we utilize an analytical framework similar to that outlined by Oomen and van den Berg (2014), particularly focusing on the manner in which rights are invoked by these actors. Initially, it becomes evident from the interview data that human rights are explicitly invoked. Primarily, this group comprises municipal councilors aligned with left-leaning political ideologies, who openly champion the human rights of immigrants/refugees (14/01/21 P12; 14/01/21 P13; 08/03/21 P21; 11/03/21 P23), or develop a narrative highlighting a dual infringement of human rights by addressing the rights of immigrants/refugees exclusively or juxtaposing them with those of Indigenous islanders (08/03/21 P21). Additionally, there are narratives acknowledging the cultural disparities among immigrants and advocating for the imperative of respecting their diverse cultural backgrounds (14/01/21 P12; 14/01/21 P13). Furthermore, the prevailing narrative paradigm that advocates for the rights of asylum seekers finds support among stakeholders engaged in nongovernmental organizations operating within the migration sector, as well as independent individuals (18/11/20 P2; 19/11/20 P3; 25/11/20 P4; 01/12/20 P6; 01/12/20 P7; 03/12/20 P8). This includes freelance collaborators associated with the Ministry of Immigration and Asylum, who emphasize the importance of upholding a balance of human rights for all individuals directly involved in this context, describing the preservation of human rights as a daily battleground (26/01/21 P17).

> Human rights constitute a daily battleground for their implementation and the application of the existing institutional framework. While facing a restrictive government policy, the reality persists with immigrants and refugees arriving in the EU, seeking acknowledgment. The defense of human rights and adherence to international law is a collective effort involving various stakeholders such as local and national authorities, the EU, NGOs and civil society. As citizens, we also share responsibility, as incidents of racism and xenophobia within various centers and regions of Greece concerning foreigners have emerged in recent years. This ongoing struggle involves ensuring the implementation of rights alongside maintaining orderly social life in

DOI: 10.4324/9781003468134-20

> destination countries. There's a continual endeavor to establish policies that strike a balance between the rights of foreigners, fair reception procedures and integration in the host countries if accepted. It's a struggle in which we all participate, even through our choices at the ballot box.
>
> (26/01/21 P17)

Furthermore, a reference to rights arises in the discourse regarding violations of the rights of island residents due to the existence of the Reception and Identification Centers (RICs). This reference is articulated by municipal councilors associated with centrist and/or right-wing political affiliations, as well as specific mayoral figures within the island's governance hierarchy, or by professionals working within the field (19/11/20 P3; 30/11/20 P5; 18/02/21 P18; 25/02/21 P20; 09/03/21 P22; 12/03/21 P24; 26/03/21 P25). In this context, an indirect allusion is made to the infringement upon the right to private property, stemming from the utilization of private land by asylum seekers necessitated by the overcrowding in RICs. Within this framework, private properties are subject to destruction, prompting legislative measures by the state to provide compensation to affected residents for damages incurred on their adjacent lands, such as olive fields (26/01/21 P17).

Second, human rights have been indirectly invoked in narratives. Municipal councilors and mayors from centrist and right-wing factions indirectly focus on human rights violations of the islanders and their narrative is related to the legal approach regarding private property rights. Furthermore, human rights indirectly manifest in narratives emphasizing the protection of rights related to health and education, as well as the promotion of solidarity toward asylum seekers. For instance, local actors emphasize the importance of solidarity toward asylum seekers, a sentiment evident not only in islands like Lesvos, Cos, Chios and Samos but particularly pronounced in places like Leros, celebrated for its unique history of hosting vulnerable groups (01/12/20 P6, 23/02/21 P19; 11/03/21 P23). Narratives highlight the challenges in offering formal education to refugee minors in Cos, a deficit partially addressed by NGOs, although not perceived as an ideal solution (22/12/20 P10). Meanwhile, the establishment of a school for refugees and asylum seekers in Lesvos serves as an example of solidarity, as it is achieved through collaborative efforts involving both refugees and members of the local community. Notably, in Lesvos international organizations and local volunteers expanded healthcare provisions to encompass pregnant women, children and those afflicted by COVID-19 (11/03/21 P23). In Chios, due to the limited capacity of the RIC, healthcare rights are safeguarded by nongovernmental organizations and the island's public hospital, which have taken on the responsibility of addressing the healthcare needs of asylum seekers (14/01/21 P12). On Samos, the public hospital bears the responsibility for delivering healthcare to asylum seekers, despite facing challenges such as limited personnel and insufficient infrastructure (P4). In the mentioned narratives, there is an implicit reference to the principles and tenets of human rights.

Third, certain narratives either explicitly or implicitly disregard human rights due to a lack of knowledge. The interviews reveal instances where some actors abstained from taking a stance on certain issues due to their limited understanding. For instance, a local actor in Lesvos explicitly stated their inability to assess the impact of the EU–Turkey Statement, arguing that it falls outside the jurisdiction of local governance, hence deeming it 'not their business' and therefore refraining from expressing an opinion. Moreover, only a minority of interviewees raised concerns regarding the practice of 'pushbacks' of refugees either from the Aegean sea waters or from the shores of the islands. Some actors, predating the widespread coverage of the pushback scandal (as reported by The Guardian in May 2022), mentioned as early as December 2020 testimonies of refoulements from the Aegean to Turkey. However, the majority of interviewees did not report any rights violations associated with the 'pushbacks' of refugees in the Aegean.

Moreover, the analysis of the narratives of local actors follows Miellet's approach. According to Miellet (2019), local actors can invoke human rights in various contexts. In doing so, a local actor may ground their narrative in different bases. For instance, some may explicitly or implicitly adopt a humanitarian perspective on rights, while others might focus solely on the legal aspects. Meanwhile, certain actors may approach rights through a pragmatic lens. In the humanitarian approach, local actors focus on the human rights of migrants and refugees. This category, which encompasses local actors in Chios (03/12/20 P8; 14/01/21 P12; 14/01/21 P13), Lesvos (11/03/21 P23), Samos (18/11/20 P2; 25/11/20 P4) and narratives concerning all the islands (26/01/21 P17).

In the legal approach, the narratives of local actors focus on both the rights of immigrants/refugees and the rights of the island's inhabitants. This category includes narratives from all islands where Refugee and Migrant RICs are established, such as Samos (08/03/21 P21) and Lesvos (21/01/21 P14; 12/03/21 P24; 13/11/20 P1). The pragmatic approach is mainly adopted by the mayors of the islands, who primarily emphasize the interests and benefits of their constituents, as well as the economy and tourism of the island (26/03/21 P25).

The narratives of various actors indirectly allude to the violation of Article 3 of the European Convention on Human Rights (ECHR), which prohibits torture and inhuman or degrading treatment. As detailed, RICs suffer from overcrowding, inadequate facilities and poor hygiene conditions. Medical care is insufficient and instances of physical violence have been reported, thereby compromising the physical safety of individuals within these facilities. Vulnerable groups are particularly susceptible to experiencing torture and violence and their residence in such conditions can exacerbate existing mental or physical health issues or induce psychological distress.

> In practice, the administration of the RIC lacks control over what occurs outside its premises, as evidenced in Samos and Moria. The situation is deemed uncontrollable due to various factors, including illegal activities. Individuals residing outside the RIC are not subject to supervision by the authorities. Often, only a few NGOs have the capacity to provide assistance. How do these individuals meet their needs? How are the nutritional requirements of these individuals calculated? This poses a significant challenge for RIC

Table 14.1 Challenges according to the narratives of local actors. Social impact/ethical issues due to the RIC

Social impact and ethical issues.
• Inadequate medical care in the RICs burdens the already insufficient structures of the hospitals at the islands. • The existence of RICs creates a division between 'locals' and 'others', between 'members' and 'nonmembers' of the societies (the separation is obvious and concerns the local level, not the state level). • Decrease in seasonal tourism, increase in permanent residents (i.e. NGOs and IOs employees, volunteers, security forces personnel). • Solidarity was replaced by xenophobia due to the 'hotspot approach' and the 'geographical limitation' imposed. New local narratives: • Asylum seekers are described as 'invaders' who will alter Greek culture. • Islamization of the Greek islands. • Ironically asylum seekers are described as 'investors'. • These narratives vary according to each island. • The geographical location of the islands affects the national consciousness of the inhabitants (the proximity of North Aegean islands to Turkey). • Solidarity varies on different islands, due to different historical and social characteristics of the islands (e.g. familiarity with different groups of people in Leros – in the past, political prisoners, mental hospital inmates). • In different narratives, the obligation of local actors to promote solidarity toward asylum seekers is emphasized.

Source: Author's compilation.

> administrators to address. Furthermore, the scarcity of medical professionals exacerbates the strain on the island's hospitals. Vulnerable groups such as minors and women are particularly at risk, highlighting the dire state of affairs.
>
> (26/01/21 P17)

The lives and human rights of asylum seekers who are obliged to live outside of the official RIC facilities are in limbo, as nobody is able to control the situation in this area. Namely, asylum seekers staying there are vulnerable to different human rights infringements. Legally, the United Nations High Commissioner for Refugees has no authority to provide assistance to those living in shacks and tents in olive groves and forests outside the official RICs. However, if and only if requested by the Greek authorities and the European Union, the High Commissioner may carry out supporting actions, such as providing tents, toilets, showers and containers, as well as implementing 'winterization' actions by supplying nonedible items like blankets, in the affected areas (21/01/21P14).

Based on the narratives provided by local actors who participated in the interviews conducted for this research, the following tables present an overview of the prevailing social impacts and ethical considerations. In the second table, these narratives from local actors are interpreted in the context of legal rights (Tables 14.1 and 14.2).

Table 14.2 Translating the narratives of local actors into a legal vocabulary

Translating narratives into legal provisions I: Violations of human rights law due to the existence of the RICs on the islands.

Issues regarding the human rights of asylum seekers

Overcrowded RICs, hygiene rule noncompliance, physical violence undermining the safety of those residing in the RICs.

Inadequate medical care, refoulement and/or pushbacks, inadequate education of minors, poor nutrition, people who arrive on the islands have become victims of 'trafficking' or 'slave trade', often associated with or facilitated by migrant smuggling.

Human rights violations of asylum seekers

- **Art. 3, ECHR**: prohibition of torture or inhuman or degrading treatment or punishment.
- **Art. 4, ECHR: prohibition of slavery and forced labour.**
- **Art. 2, Prot. No. 1, ECHR: right to education.**
- **Art. 5 ECHR: right to liberty and security.**
- **Art. 33 of the 1951 Refugee Convention**: prohibition of expulsion or return ('refoulement').

Issues concerning the human rights of inhabitants of the islands

Violation of the right to property of the inhabitants due to the overcrowded official RIC and the use of land for setting up tents and shelters.

Violation of the right to private and family life due to inadequate sanitary conditions and the nuisance in the area.

Human rights violations of the inhabitants of the island

- **Art. 8, ECHR: right to respect for private and family life.**
- **Art. 1, Prot.** No. **1, ECHR**: protection of property.

Translating narratives into legal provisions II: Social justice through solidarity.
The glocalization of human rights or the preservation of human rights through solidarity actions by local residents, volunteers, NGOs, lawyers and municipal councilors directed at asylum seekers in RICs on the islands.

Safeguarding the rights of asylum seekers

- **Art. 13, ECHR**: right to an effective remedy.
- **Art. 2, Prot. No. 1, ECHR**: right to education.

Safeguarding the rights of the inhabitants of the islands:

- **Art. 8, ECHR**: right to respect for private and family life.

Source: Author's compilation.

15 Human rights fulfillment at the local level

Glocalisation and vernacularization of human rights through social justice and solidarity

The glocalization of human rights entails a 'vernacularized' approach, elucidating the manner in which human rights norms and principles undergo implementation, translation and contestation at the grassroots level (Merry 2006). The central tenet of this approach lies in the notion that global norms are interpreted and applied by actors who blur the distinct boundary between 'global' and 'local'. These actors may include mayors, municipal councilors, human rights lawyers or local activists (Merry 2006; Resnik 2007; Miellet 2019, pp. 214–215). Functioning as a mechanism, human rights facilitate the engagement and mobilization of diverse interest groups, fostering support for inclusive initiatives aimed at achieving social justice (Connolly 2005, cited in Darling 2016, p. 158). However, although human rights offer a distinctive alternative narrative to existing power imbalances, structural inequality and injustice, experiences observed at the local level worldwide illustrate that transforming these principles into municipal policies is a challenging endeavor (Fernández-Wulff 2023). Parallel to this, European Union (EU) policies regarding migrants underscore a prevalent approach where the challenges posed by a refugee crisis are often addressed through policies rather than legal frameworks. This dynamic creates a scenario where virtually everything, including the protection of refugees, becomes subject to negotiation (Goodwin-Gill 1999, p. 240, as quoted in Gammeltoft-Hansen 2014, p. 574). The assertion has been highlighted that the European refugee crisis can be construed as a manifestation of a crisis within the governance paradigm of the EU concerning asylum policies (Ponzo 2022, p. 39).

Academics have emphasized the rise in various procedural and physical deterrent measures over the past 25 years in both longstanding and recently established asylum nations. Not only have illegal pushbacks occurred, but legal methods to circumvent refugee flows have also been employed. Various strategies and tactics have been implemented in both Europe and North America to mitigate the influx of voluminous asylum applications. In the European context, a significant strategy materialized with the introduction of the Dublin Convention in 1997. The convention, replaced by the Dublin III Regulation (Regulation (EU) No 604/2013), advocated for redirecting asylum claims to the first safe country of entry. Additionally, distinct tactics have been devised to delineate the nuanced interpretation of terms such as 'territory' and 'borders' pertaining to a state. In the prevailing context, certain states have formally asserted that zones encompassing airports or

DOI: 10.4324/9781003468134-21

other ingress points situated along their borders fall outside the purview of their sovereign territory, thus precluding the submission of asylum requests within these areas. Employing this stratagem, these states contend that their actions, including the repatriation of individuals from such points without due consideration or examination of their asylum requests, do not contravene the nonrefoulement principle stipulated in the Geneva Convention. This contention persists even when individuals declare refugee status. Notably, instances have been documented where vessels transporting refugees were intercepted and prevented from continuing their maritime passage (Carens 2013, p. 199).

Some scholars have characterized these policies as unfolding 'beyond legal constraints', within a 'legal vacuum' or in a metaphorical 'legal black hole' (Vandvik 2008, p. 28). In the same vein, a narrative in Lesvos emphasizes that EU migration policies applied at the Reception and Identification Centers (RICs) on the Greek islands circumvent the provisions of the Geneva Convention without abolishing the legal text. The EU implements policies related to RICs on islands, even if these policies may be perceived as violating the Geneva Convention, which has not been formally revoked. An example of this violation is highlighted by the prolonged stay of asylum seekers in temporary status within the asylum centers on the islands. Additionally, if these individuals later obtain refugee status, they are reportedly not included in integration programs, contrary to stipulations in international and European legislation regarding asylum examination time limits and integration procedures for recognized refugees. The narrative suggests that despite the inconsistency of EU migration policies with human rights standards, alternative approaches are being pursued, potentially involving the application of laws that may be considered unconstitutional, exploiting the fact that the Geneva Convention has not been officially repealed (11/03/21 P23). In this milieu, the diminutive Greek islands find themselves compelled to adhere to the repercussions of EU policies. This situation is juxtaposed with the reluctance of certain governments across various EU countries to engage in the relocation of asylum seekers from Greece and Italy (Sabchev 2021b).

In this scenario, in 2016, the refugee crisis was characterized by the then-United Nations Secretary-General Ban Ki-moon as a solidarity crisis, emphasizing the deficiency of support for refugees from EU member states (Sabchev 2022, p. 2). Individual states exhibit a lack of solidarity with refugees and there is a deficiency in international or intergovernmental unity when addressing the repercussions of forced displacement. For example, countries like Hungary and Austria blatantly disregard refugee distribution (Segarra 2023; 08/03/21 P21). All in all, despite the legal provisions stemming from international and humanitarian law, states often fail to adhere to international refugee and human rights law. In contradistinction to this trend, amidst the initial surge of refugee movements, a multitude of local entities within the tiny Greek islands that host asylum centers, exhibited solidarity with asylum seekers. Alongside the official aid provided by national governments and organizations at the international level, informal groups, individual volunteers and grassroots NGOs have also stepped up to provide assistance outside the formal frameworks of international organizations like the United Nations.

Amidst the escalating refugee influx in 2015–2016, the local residents undertook initiatives closely tied to the 'vernacularization' of human rights for asylum seekers, as evidenced by a noteworthy surge in solidarity actions across all five islands. In all the islands examined in this research, the vernacularization of human rights is evident in the narratives of local actors. It manifests through the active engagement of numerous individuals whether of Greek or foreign origin, autonomously demonstrating solidarity by providing aid to refugees. Additionally, municipal and nongovernmental actors participate in this vernacularization. Remarkably intriguing are initiatives that distinctly involve asylum seekers, encouraging their active participation in solidarity endeavors. In this context, the existence of RICs on the Aegean islands exemplifies the idea of the 'vernacularization' of human rights. Local actors, in the course of their daily lives, interface intimately with asylum seekers, thereby assuming the role of first-hand observers amidst one of the most significant refugee influxes in contemporary history. Within this framework, the process of 'vernacularization' of human rights is investigated through a meticulous examination of the intricate dynamics involving local actors in upholding human rights and fostering solidarity toward asylum seekers. The organic emergence of local solidarity stems from the unique exigencies of the region, addressing distinct challenges that manifest in the strenuous and at times, degrading conditions prevalent at RICs.

The dynamics surrounding RICs transcend local boundaries, originating from broader European asylum policies. A prominent illustration is the 'geographic restriction' enforced since 2015, compelling asylum seekers to remain on the islands (19/11/20 P3; 22/12/20 P11; 11/03/21 P23; 13/11/20 P1; 26/03/21 P25). In this context, considering broader European asylum policies, when filtered through the lens of localized human rights, the narratives of local actors reveal contrasting discourses on the potential for the glocalization of human rights. On one hand, there is recognition of the potential for municipalities to advocate for the glocalization of human rights by exerting pressure on the government within RIC-related decision-making processes (11/18/20 P2) or when local leadership serves as a platform to politically articulate the collective will of its residents (26/03/21 P25). The municipality could direct efforts toward enhancing conditions beyond the RIC, intervening in response to issues affecting the local population or tourism (22/12/20 P11). In this narrative, the glocalization of human rights primarily revolves around safeguarding the rights of local residents. However, political expediency often leads local authorities to align with government immigration policies, potentially compromising human rights, as seen in the case of advocating for a new Closed Controlled Structure in Lesvos and the other islands, despite local opposition (11/03/21 P23). On the other hand, in certain instances, municipal authorities exhibit direct opposition to refugee populations. An illustrative case is observed in the stance of the mayor of Chios, whose alignment with right-wing political ideology is manifested through the public articulation of anti-refugee sentiments. This stance denotes a prevailing reluctance to accommodate refugees within the jurisdiction of Chios and a notable absence of proactive measures aimed at ameliorating their living conditions (03/12/20 P8). While local authorities may fail to address refugee issues in certain instances and notwithstanding the potential political agency municipalities possess in expressing the collective will of their residents, governmental disregard for decisions made by municipal councils, as observed in locales such as Leros, raises pertinent concerns regarding the efficacy of local influence in shaping asylum policies and safeguarding human rights at the grassroots level (23/02/21 P19).

Nevertheless, local actors, including volunteers and NGO personnel, wield significant influence in ameliorating living conditions within asylum centers and tackling broader issues affecting local populations (11/19/20 P3). This collective effort contributes to the glocalization of human rights endeavors. However, it's crucial to note that some narratives from local actors underscore the contentious presence of NGOs. These narratives reveal that certain local citizens harbor a negative perception of NGOs, viewing them with suspicion due to perceived economic motivations (09/03/21 P22). In all the islands hosting RICs, only officially registered organizations are authorized to help within the RICs. Nevertheless, initiatives or NGOs lacking official registration did exist, exclusively providing services outside the RICs or may engage in collaboration with officially registered NGOs. Solidarity permeated the fabric of community life among residents, volunteers and various collectives throughout the islands under scrutiny, namely Cos, Chios, Lesvos, Leros and Samos.

In Lesvos, a myriad of organizations actively engage in initiatives associated with refugee solidarity. For instance, local support manifested in diverse ways, such as humanitarian aid offered by residents (13/11/20 P1; 26/03/21 P25), the organization 'Coexistence and Communication in the Aegean' ('Synyparxi kai Epikoinwnia sto Aigaio') and the collaborative endeavors of 'Solidarity for All' ('Allileggyi gia Olous'), providing humanitarian aid outside the Moria Lesvos structure, in the area called 'Olive Grove' ('Elaionas') (11/03/21 P23). Since asylum seekers were obliged to reside outside the official asylum center due to the limited capacity, the 'Olive Grove' emerges beyond the confines of the official RIC in Moria. Within this domain, described as being 'in the middle of this chaos', individuals fashioned their own microcosms, cultivating flowers and perhaps even small gardens. Amidst this environment, solidarity initiatives flourished, manifesting in the creation of schools that catered to educational needs of refugees (11/03/21 P23). Moreover, notably, in Lesvos, the Municipal Refugee Center in Kara Tepe, distinct from the RIC, has been characterized by various local actors as an exemplary facility, despite its scheduling for closure. In line with this, a paradigmatic illustration unfolded with the accommodation facility for asylum seekers and refugees at PIKPA camp, hailed by local actors as an embodiment of a 'dignified structure'. It was extolled as 'something unprecedented at the European level', distinct from any comparable establishment, showcasing a unique form of self-organization. Within its premises, a fully functional school and kindergarten operated, distinguishing it markedly from conventional RICs. Nevertheless, despite its distinguished attributes, the PIKPA facility met closure in October 2020, necessitating the relocation of its inhabitants to Mavrovouni RIC (11/03/21 P23; 13/11/20 P1).

Parallel to these entities and initiatives, in Lesvos, local residents demonstrate tangible solidarity by expressing genuine interest and aiding, such as offering clothing and food. Notably, some have extended their hospitality by opening their homes to host individuals for short stays, exemplified during vacation occasions. The core idea of a narration is that while the state bears primary responsibility for addressing certain needs, such as providing education for refugee children, there is also a collective responsibility within society to fill gaps in services. This is exemplified by the positive role played by private initiatives and grassroots mobilization in addressing humanitarian challenges, as seen in Lesvos (11/13/20 P1). Indeed, the local society of Lesvos demonstrated generosity by providing all possible material support. Artistic endeavors thrived, with local or foreign artists creating and painters expressing their craft, while musicians formed groups. However, amidst this harmonious coexistence, there were also groups that sought to manipulate asylum seekers, exploiting their vulnerability by making deceptive promises to secure necessary documents for onward travel to other European countries (11/03/21 P23).

In Samos, in narrative, it is pointed out that with the focus predominantly directed toward Lesvos, other islands such as Samos have not received widespread attention in the context of the refugee crisis. Consequently, there is a limited presence of NGOs on Samos relative to the considerable needs prevailing on the island (25/11/20 P4). However, various solidarity initiatives exist, though, they have decreased over the years. In addition to NGOs, a significant volunteer-led effort is the 'Anti-racist Initiative'. The surge in the RIC population of Samos in 2015 prompted a significant portion of services to be outsourced to NGOs, leading to a professionalization of activities within the RIC. Paradoxically, this professionalization was observed to create a distancing effect, eroding the sense of solidarity among individuals (03/08/21 P21). In the initial three years, solidarity groups were present, yet their prevalence gradually diminished over time (12/03/21 P24). The integration of asylum seekers into the local community of Samos encountered obstacles and the presence of the asylum center emerged as a source of exhaustion for the local population. Tensions within the RIC, occasionally resulting in acts of arson, contributed to a climate of fear and frustration among the local community (18/11/20 P2).

In Cos, the well-known Arvanitakis, the baker, has gained global recognition for his altruistic efforts toward refugees. Arvanitakis's inclusive support is highlighted by local narratives, extending assistance to both asylum seekers and local residents (22/12/20 P10). According to the narrative of the head of the RIC, in Cos, there is a smooth collaboration among the RIC administration in Cos, with the municipality, the Region, the Port Authority and civic organizations on the island as long as they are accredited (08/05/21 P27). NGOs like Arsis contribute to the education of minor refugees, both in Cos and in Leros, with initiatives benefiting from the involvement of both staff and volunteers, some of whom are refugees themselves. Additionally, during the field research period, NGOs like 'Flying Help' operated on Cos, comprising a collaborative effort between local residents and individuals from Germany or the Netherlands who chose to reside on the island due to their affinity for it (22/12/20 P10). In the municipality of Cos, initiatives of solidarity emanating from local leadership predominantly align with the objective of safeguarding the interests and human rights germane to the local community. In accordance with this particular narrative, the municipal authority endeavors to provide assistance with the intention of fostering conditions within the RIC that are deemed acceptably humane. A notable instance of such intervention is discerned in the proactive involvement of the municipality of Cos in matters pertaining to hygiene, expressly directed toward ameliorating the health and living conditions of the individuals residing in the RIC. This commitment was particularly evident during the heightened influx of asylum seekers before the onset of the coronavirus pandemic in 2019–2020. The municipality actively engaged in the sanitation of the RIC area, employing machinery to transfer certain asylum seekers from peripheral shelters encircling the RIC to locations within the RIC structure itself (18/02/21 P18).

In Cos, in the same vein as other islands, the municipal authority's provision of aid is not solely driven by a desire to 'relieve tension' for asylum seekers; rather, it is strategically oriented toward instilling a sense of security among the locals, colloquially referred to as 'our people'. In essence, the overarching objective is to effectively manage overpopulation dynamics within the RIC, ensuring that the local community perceives a proactive approach that mitigates potential sources of insecurity (18/02/21 P18). This narrative refrains from invoking the human rights framework in relation to asylum seekers, instead centering its attention on the community of Cos and prioritizing the economic and social interests specific to the local populace. Notably, a conspicuous demarcation emerges between the categorizations of 'locals' and 'others', as evidenced by the use of terms such as 'ours' and 'people of Cos'. Such delineations align with 'partiality' approaches, as has been expounded upon in the previous chapters.

In Chios, during the onset of the main refugee crisis in 2015–2016, some local residents demonstrated hospitality by accommodating asylum seekers in their homes (25/02/21 P20). Simultaneously, asylum seekers predominantly found temporary residence in the city center garden, where noteworthy solidarity initiatives were observed, involving both local residents and volunteers. Various services, including a social kitchen, were provided during that period and these actions were undertaken in collaboration with the municipality in Chios (14/01/21 P12). However, during the period of the interviews, the local leadership of Chios ceased collaboration with any of the solidarity collectivities (14/01/21 P12; 25/02/21 P20).

On the other hand, Leros, due to its distinctive history of providing shelter to vulnerable populations and the relatively limited influx of asylum seekers to the island, has been characterized in narratives by various actors as an exemplary model of RICs. The vernacularization of human rights manifested in instances of solidarity with refugees, particularly during the initial phases of the refugee influx from 2015 to 2017, facilitated through collaboration between local political leadership, NGOs and independent individuals. In the initial surge of refugee influx, Leros inhabitants and the church provided assistance to asylum seekers. As per the director of the RIC in Leros, the municipal political leadership consistently extends assistance to refugees, including support within the asylum center premises, such as involvement in waste management initiatives (09/05/21 P28). The glocalization of human rights, as a process, finds realization through the endeavors of individuals who actively seek to effectuate change, directing their efforts toward collective and organized initiatives. The central objective revolves around discerning the individual agency of professionals and their capacity to instigate transformative change. In a local narrative, while voluntary contributions represent commendable gestures, they prove insufficient in addressing the substantive challenges inherent in this context. A more comprehensive, collective and organized effort is requisite, one that extends beyond immediate aid to encompass a strategic focus on policy advocacy concerning refugees (22/01/21 P16).

Despite demonstrating profound solidarity and extending generous assistance to refugees, their altruistic efforts were so substantial that, for example, the residents of Lesvos were considered for a Nobel Peace Prize (26/03/21 P25). However, over an extended period, the continuous strain of this humanitarian endeavor eventually took its toll, leading to a palpable sense of weariness among the local population (26/03/21 P25). The rapid escalation in numbers precipitated a sense of fatigue, resulting in heightened societal tensions and a diminishing of empathic sentiments. Presently, a prevailing sentiment among the majority is a desire for the departure of a substantial portion of the refugees, acknowledging the challenges posed by the disruptions, insecurities and societal divisions. In the context of the five Greek islands under scrutiny, the process of vernacularization pertaining to human rights appears to emanate predominantly from the collective endeavors of local inhabitants, municipal council members, volunteers, NGO personnel and to a limited extent, sporadic initiatives by local political leadership. Simultaneously, the vernacularized rights encounter a diminishing trajectory influenced by EU policies (26/01/21 P17) and the concomitant frustration experienced by the populace residing on these islands, thereby detrimentally impacting the solidarity with refugees. The requirement to process asylum requests entirely on the Greek islands led to prolonged stays in overcrowded reception facilities marked by inadequate conditions. This setting became a conducive environment for the routine violation of migrants' human rights. The initial expressions of solidarity among local actors waned as residents grew fatigued and perceived the situation as unjust, having to witness such degrading conditions (08/03/21 P21). As a consequence, sentiments of societal solidarity waned, replaced by a prevailing sense of apathy. Individuals who initially exhibited helpfulness underwent a transformation, evolving from benevolence to palpable frustration (11/03/21 P23). From the narratives, it becomes apparent, that the vernacularisation of human rights is undermined due to the division of the local community. In the islands, residents are divided into two categories: those who express solidarity and the rest. In Chios for example, during the period the interviews were conducted, the former group attempted to burn down the warehouse where Chios Solidarity had collected materials for solidarity, such as clothing and food, considering them an enemy of the homeland. This stance was intensified by criminal actions of refugees, provoking the community's reaction. Friends of refugees were deemed unpatriotic, reinforcing prejudices and xenophobia (03/12/20 P8).

Nevertheless, earnest endeavors are underway to engage in measured discussions and proactively tackle refugee-related concerns. This includes concerted efforts toward fostering the integration of those refugees who opt to remain on the island (11/03/21 P23). Local actors underscore the limited scope for action at the local level while citing instances of municipalities in Greece that have successfully implemented commendable practices pertaining to refugees. Illustratively, the municipality of Tilos is cited, wherein the local authority demonstrated solidarity by integrating refugees into the community, addressing economic and employment challenges, resulting in the absence of racist phenomena. Concurrently, Tilos maintains exemplary performance in tourism, culture and alternative energy sectors. According to narratives from actors, local leadership plays a pivotal role in shaping public opinion and educating the community. Consequently, a municipality that embodies solidarity, respects human rights and presents a humanitarian ethos is posited to foster positive conditions within the local society.

Despite the exhaustion experienced by local residents and the waning of solidarity efforts, coupled with narratives highlighting perceived constraints on local action, there are still a number of initiatives that persisted in offering support to refugees. These initiatives collectively contribute to the process of vernacularizing human rights. It is noteworthy that, in this context, there is a 'glocalization' of human rights, manifested through the emergence of numerous initiatives from local entities. This emphasizes the intricate connection where human rights can either be realized or jeopardized. Within this complex constellation, these islands emerge as pivotal arenas of contestation and connection (Darling 2016, p. 170). The establishment of RICs on the islands underscores the relocation of 'frames of human rights' to these specific locales, as articulated by Darling (2016, p. 157), notably converging on the island hotspots. Concurrently, local actors, both knowingly and unknowingly, interface with human rights law and norms when undertaking initiatives in the field. The salience of human rights lies in their capacity to articulate a universal language and vision that extends beyond local confines. Across the five Greek islands where asylum centers are located, the 'vernacularization' of human rights manifests itself. 'Vernacularized' human rights delineate the perception and implementation of human rights within local communities, accounting for the capacities and benevolent motivations of those actively involved in championing human rights and expressing solidarity with asylum seekers. This process also sheds light on the constraints or, in certain instances, the presence of antagonistic dispositions among select individuals within the local milieu.

Solidarity endeavors that exemplify the 'vernacularization' of human rights and the 'glocalization' of rights can be referred to as 'good practices'. These practices align with facets of impartialism, specifically resonating with the principles of global liberalism and egalitarianism. Global liberalism fundamentally relies on the discourse of rights, emphasizing our ethical responsibilities to those in vulnerable circumstances. Refusal to provide shelter not only entails complicity in ongoing injustice but also entails shared moral culpability for its perpetuation. Similarly, aspects of egalitarianism overlap with solidarity actions. Within the framework of luck egalitarianism, solidarity becomes intricately connected to the pursuit of distributive justice. The primary objective of any distributive principle, in this context, is to mitigate the repercussions of arbitrary luck on an individual's overall well-being. On the flip side, an alternative perspective of egalitarianism contends that the principal objective resides in attenuating the capricious influence of fortune in the allocation of commodities and resources among individuals within the societal framework. The principles of global liberalism and egalitarianism, encompassed within the framework of impartialism, provide valuable guidelines for the development of local policies aimed at protecting the human rights of marginalized populations, notably refugees and advancing social justice. In this context, narratives articulated by local actors who align with impartiality and those local actors who actively engage in solidarity actions, become instructive in the glocalization of human rights. Specifically, these discernible local actors, characterized as 'significant human rights theorists', adhere to principles of global liberalism and egalitarianism as they contribute to the actualization of human rights glocalization in practice.

Nevertheless, while local entities' initiatives are vital, they alone cannot shoulder the responsibility for refugee support. Municipal authorities must actively engage in addressing refugee issues and advocate for a more significant role in this regard. Simultaneously, international cooperation is crucial for addressing what are commonly referred to as global public goods. Refugee protection, for instance, can be seen as a global or regional public good, benefiting multiple states regardless of their individual contributions. Similarly, addressing the root causes of displacement and implementing lasting solutions can offer nonexcludable benefits to states, enhancing security and fulfilling humanitarian goals for several states (Betts 2009, p. 80). Therefore, akin to proposals for international collaboration among states, there is a pressing need for international cooperation among municipal authorities grappling with similar refugee flows. Such collaboration would facilitate the exchange of experiences, articulation of shared challenges and dissemination of best practices. These concerted efforts are essential for promoting the vernacularization of human rights at the grassroots level, ensuring that the principles of dignity and protection are upheld universally while they are allocated locally.

Conclusion

The present research reveals that human rights play a central role explicitly or implicitly in the narratives of local actors regarding the Reception and Identification Centers (RICs) in the Aegean. When translating the narratives of local actors into a 'legal vocabulary', specifically within the framework of positive law and established human rights law, both explicit and implicit instances of rights violations and protections become apparent. More specifically, human rights find expression in narratives highlighting the safeguarding of health and education rights, coupled with the advocacy for solidarity toward asylum seekers. Noteworthy instances of solidarity are evident in islands such as Lesvos, Cos, Chios and Samos, as well as in places like Leros, renowned for hosting vulnerable groups. Challenges in providing formal education to refugee minors in Cos are acknowledged, with nongovernmental organizations addressing the deficit, though not deemed an ideal solution. Collaborative efforts in Lesvos led to the establishment of schools for minors and asylum seekers, involving refugees and the local community. Additionally, Lesvos saw international organizations and local volunteers extending healthcare services to vulnerable groups such as pregnant women, children and those affected by COVID-19. In Chios, constrained by the asylum center's capacity, nongovernmental organizations and the public hospital assumed responsibility for addressing asylum seekers' healthcare needs. Similarly, in Samos, the public hospital undertakes healthcare duties for asylum seekers despite challenges in personnel and infrastructure.

In all of these islands, solidarity was apparent among local inhabitants, volunteers and community groups. For example, in Lesvos, local support took various forms, including humanitarian aid provided by local inhabitants (13/11/20 P1; 26/03/21 P25), the association 'Coexistence and Communication in the Aegean' ('Synyparxi kai Epikoinwnia sto Aigaio') and the collective effort of 'Solidarity for All' (11/03/21 P23). In Leros, acts of solidarity were initiated by the 'Leros Solidarity Network', comprising individuals from Europe and the USA, or facilitated through the philanthropic efforts of the Metropolis of Leros (09/03/21 P22). In Chios, existing solidarity initiatives include 'Chios Solidarity' and the 'Antivaro' social organization, wherein certain actions involve participation from left-wing-oriented municipal councilors (14/01/21 P12). Furthermore, in Cos, Leros and Lesvos, municipal authorities have consistently provided support to

DOI: 10.4324/9781003468134-22

sanitation services, engaging in waste collection within asylum centers, beyond their official mandates (18/02/21 P18; 23/02/21 P19; 11/03/21 P23). This initiative is driven by dual objectives, namely safeguarding local residents in proximity to the RICs (18/02/21 P18) and expressing solidarity toward refugees (11/03/21 P23).

Additionally, in narratives, not only solidarity actions that safeguard localized rights are present, but also rights that are lost at the local level – whether implicitly or explicitly – are revealed. In narratives focusing on violations of asylum seekers' rights, the absolute right under Article 3 of the European Convention on Human Rights (ECHR) is violated. Narratives related to Article 3 of the ECHR make direct or indirect reference to the right against degrading and inhuman treatment, the obligation to provide free medical care to asylum seekers, as well as the inability to protect vulnerable groups. Reference is made to the violation of Article 4 of the ECHR, as local actors explicitly mention that asylum seekers approaching the Aegean islands fall victim to trafficking/exploitation due to illegal migrant smuggling for the financial benefit of traffickers. Furthermore, in the narratives, a violation of Article 2, Protocol No. 1 of the ECHR, which concerns the right to education, is identified. Local actors explicitly state that the right of refugee children to receive education in public school structures on the islands is being undermined.

The violation of Article 5 of the ECHR, namely the right to liberty and security, is highlighted. In certain narratives, the 'geographical restriction' on the islands and the prolonged stay of asylum seekers in facilities such as the RICs violate the right to freedom of movement. In many narratives, the asylum centers are characterized as 'detention centers' with a 'punitive' character. Moreover, in most narratives of local actors from all islands, there is mention of the 'entrapment' of asylum seekers on the islands, aiming to send a clear deterrent message to halt refugee flows. Furthermore, there is a violation of Article 33 of the Geneva Convention, which is the principle of nonrefoulement for those seeking international protection. The violation of this provision is related to both illegal refoulements to Turkey and the 'externalization of EU policies' regarding migration, including the EU–Turkey Agreement, which entails deportation to Turkey, considered a 'safe third country'.

Additionally, in narratives of local actors, violations of the rights of the island residents emerge. As these narratives are 'translated into legal terminology', these violations are related to the violation of Article 8 of the ECHR, which concerns the right to respect for private and family life. This right is violated due to the establishment of structures on the islands where hygiene rules are not observed, leading to overcrowding and disturbance, as the number of asylum seekers has exceeded the capacity of the structures. The overcrowding of the facilities has also led to the violation of Article 1, Protocol No. 1 of the ECHR regarding the protection of individual property, as people are forced to live in tents and makeshift settlements on private property outside the official structure. Simultaneously, there are delays from the competent authorities regarding compensating residents for the use of their property covering the deficiencies of the RICs. Finally, one of the main findings of the research is that the human rights of asylum seekers are explicitly or implicitly disregarded in narratives that prioritize concepts such as 'national sovereignty', 'local economy', 'local interest' and 'public safety of the local community'. The prioritization of the rights and interests of the citizens of the local community is closely associated with these concepts. The main findings of the research derive from narratives that have been meticulously scrutinized through the analytical lens of metaphors and myths, revealing significant insights into the subject matter. Specifically, the narratives employ the following metaphors and myths:

a Chios (Vial): the RIC in Chios is depicted as a 'concentration camp' or a 'slum', with its concept labeled as 'punitive' and 'inhumane'. RICs are referred to as 'punitive concentration camps' and the islands hosting them are described as 'fortress islands' or 'prison islands'. Due to the limited capacity of the RIC, nongovernmental organizations and the public hospital shoulder the responsibility for catering to the healthcare needs of asylum seekers. Some local elected officials present themselves as 'refugee fighters' aiming to solve the refugee problem. Asylum seekers in Chios are ironically labeled as 'investors' or 'illegal immigrants as invaders', accused of seeking to 'alter our culture' in favor of Erdogan's 'Islamization of the islands'. The EU–Turkey Agreement of 2016 is viewed as a 'key point' or 'turning point' for asylum seekers and the local community, creating 'double borders' for Chios residents and using the 'sea as a border' to confine asylum seekers on the islands. Political decisions by the EU and Greek governments are seen as strengthening the extreme right, with the islands metaphorically transformed into 'prisons' after the agreement. Following the experience in Vial, there is reluctance to have the asylum center 'in their backyard'. Chios's identity is depicted metaphorically as a 'prison island' and a 'refugee island' due to the RIC.
b Cos, Pyli: Cos is depicted as the 'forefront' of Greece's national sovereignty in the eastern Aegean. Consequently, there is a call for its removal from the 'migration map' to prevent it from serving as the 'soft underbelly' during periods of political tension or as a target for expansionist policies aimed at occupying Greek territories. Policies aimed at stemming migration flows through enhanced border control convey a message of control to those on the other side, acting as a deterrent to both 'smugglers' and asylum seekers. The 'relationship with the neighboring country' (i.e. Turkey) and the EU's ties with Turkey are considered pivotal in addressing immigration issues. Narratives also highlight the challenges in providing formal education to refugee minors in Cos, with some alleviation of this shortfall achieved through the efforts of nongovernmental organizations.
c Leros, Lepida: the RIC in Lepida has been likened to 'another village', bearing a 'burden' that local authorities must manage, despite its disproportionate size relative to the island. The 'small island' of Leros is tasked with shouldering the 'big burden' of migration, with some narratives expressing reluctance to see the island 'stigmatized again' as in the past. The Aegean islands are described as 'trapped', while refugees and immigrants also find themselves 'trapped' in the same situation. Leros 'is mired' in a 'prolonged crisis' and faces 'marginalization' due to the migration crisis. Narratives underscore the importance of

demonstrating solidarity with asylum seekers, particularly evident on islands like Leros, renowned for their historical role in hosting vulnerable groups.

d Lesvos, Moria until Sept. 2020 and Mavrovouni or Kara Tepe: the RIC in Mavrovouni and particularly in Moria is depicted in a narrative as 'the shame of Europe'. The EU is portrayed as investing billions to prevent refugees from entering Europe and to construct 'ultra-luxurious concentration camps'. The RIC in Lesvos is likened to a 'second big city', while feelings of solidarity within society are described as being 'crushed', with a prevailing sentiment of no longer being able to accept the RIC on the island. The proposed new Closed Controlled Structures on the islands are characterized as 'superstructures' equipped with all amenities, reminiscent of the large camps accommodating millions of refugees outside Lebanon. The residents of Mytilini were once hailed as potential recipients of the Nobel Peace Prize for their solidarity with refugees, but are now described as 'tired'. The presence of the asylum center on the island is seen as imposing an 'uneven' and 'significant burden' on social, administrative and financial levels.

e Samos, Vathy: the narratives of local actors depict Samos as unable to accommodate such a large overpopulation at the asylum center, leading to the island being stigmatized. Despite this, the public hospital on Samos is tasked with providing healthcare to asylum seekers, although it faces challenges due to limited personnel and inadequate infrastructure. The islands of the eastern Aegean are portrayed as 'repositories of souls' and 'embankments', supporting the 'North of Europe' while facing daunting expenses associated with the RICs.

From this research, it becomes evident that the existence of asylum centers shapes the narratives of local actors on the islands, resulting in the assertion and relinquishment of different interests and the glocalized rights of actors belonging to various groups. On the one hand, the glocalized rights of locals are emphasized, while on the other hand, the glocalized rights of asylum seekers are highlighted. Narratives focusing on the rights of society members often reflect elements of conservatism and communitarian approaches, whereas narratives that underscore violations of asylum seekers' rights align more closely with the principles of global liberalism and egalitarianism.

Furthermore, the different categorizations and entanglements of human rights by various actors, as derived from the narratives in the interviews of the research, have been primarily grouped into three following Miellet (2019) framework. First, the humanitarian approach, where local actors focus on the human rights of migrants and refugees (this category includes municipal councilors from Chios and Lesvos). Second, the legal approach, which emphasizes the rights and obligations arising from international and European law. In this approach, narratives of local actors also focus on the rights of migrants/refugees and the rights of the island residents (here, narratives from nongovernmental organizations in Lesvos, narratives from international organizations and selected approaches in Samos can be included). Third, the pragmatic approach is primarily adopted by the mayors of the islands, who, in their narratives, mainly refer to the interests and benefits of their voters.

To the extent that international principles and values are advocated at the local level, the 'glocalization' of human rights becomes apparent. In the narratives of the actors, local communities on the islands seem to have responded to the initial refugee flows in 2015 with solidarity. The intention to assist refugees and defend their rights stemmed from humanitarian reasons and the islands were characterized by a 'pro-refugee sentiment'. However, over the years, as solutions were not found and the situation in the RICs worsened, the local community on the islands began to grow weary and their attitude shifted to a more skeptical one as they tried to understand what was happening on the islands. According to other narratives, the prolonged stay of asylum seekers in the RICs following the implementation of the 'geographical restriction' led to the end of solidarity or, at least, its weakening, while racist discourse began to emerge. The EU–Turkey Agreement played a decisive role in this, as it enforced the 'geographical restriction' on the islands, prohibited movement to the mainland and required individuals to remain on the islands until a decision was made on their asylum claims. This essentially means that a large number of asylum seekers are trapped on the islands for an extended period, in some cases reaching two years.

Another narrative found in the descriptions of local actors is the intention of municipal authorities to help solve certain problems related to RICs (e.g. waste collection, improved hygiene conditions in the RIC area, work outside RICs to install tents). According to the narratives, through these actions, local authorities aimed primarily at eliminating tensions and preventing potential conflicts within the local community. In this context, the defense of the rights of asylum seekers and residents stems from a 'pragmatic' intention aiming to absorb potential shocks within the social fabric of the islands. In these approaches, the actions taken to improve conditions in the area where the RICs are located aim to prevent tensions and protect the rights and interests of the local population. These narratives can also be linked to 'local pragmatism' (Poppelaars and Scholten 2008), which involves addressing issues to prevent the worsening of problems and avoid accusations of 'negligence' and 'lack of response' to municipal requests.

The division between the interests and rights of asylum seekers on the one hand and members of the local community, on the other hand, is central in the narratives of actors categorized either in the communitarian or conservative theoretical framework – narratives that fall within the broader stream of 'partiality'. In the narratives of these local actors, there is either indirect or direct reference to the need to primarily defend the rights of members of the local community. Narratives falling under 'impartialism', specifically within global liberalism and egalitarianism, emphasize violations of rights against asylum seekers. In these narratives, the obligations of prosperous democratic states to assist asylum seekers due to the 'causal connection' are highlighted, as well as the obligation to protect vulnerable population groups and the judgment of humanitarianism. They also point to the rise of racism and xenophobia as a result of the policies followed on the islands.

While the majority of local actors participating in the interviews are generally opposed to the RICs and specifically against the creation of new and large-capacity Closed Controlled Structures on the islands, the arguments of each actor vary. On the one hand, there are local actors falling under 'partiality' in their narratives, focusing on the negative consequences of asylum centers for tourism and prioritizing the protection of the rights and interests of members of the local community over refugees. On the other hand, there are local actors categorized under 'impartiality' who do not prioritize the rights of members of the community simply because they happen to be members of the local island community. On the contrary, the focal point of their narrative lies in the deplorable living conditions of asylum seekers residing in asylum centers and the violation of their rights. This includes the right to asylum, the right against degrading treatment, human trafficking and the labor rights of asylum seekers and refugees who fall victim to exploitation through low-cost and/or undeclared labor.

Simultaneously, narratives falling under the category of 'impartiality' involve narrations of actors referring to the 'causal connection' of obligations toward refugees and migrants. This is based on the indirect or direct involvement of states in wars and environmental destruction, creating refugee flows. In this context, the UN and the EU are obligated to protect the rights of refugees and take measures to end the 'trafficking' of refugees/migrants and drownings in the Mediterranean Sea. Narratives categorized under impartialism, along with arguments advocating for impartial approaches, can serve as guiding principles for formulating fair policies concerning refugees. Particularly, distributive justice offers insights into how resources and opportunities should be distributed within society, including to asylum seekers and refugees. Egalitarianism posits that justice necessitates individuals to have equal concern and respect for each other's rights and interests and that disparities in resource allocation due to brute luck should be rectified. Applying egalitarian principles to the context of asylum and refugee protection, it entails that societies have an obligation to ensure that the needs of asylum seekers and refugees are met in a fair and equitable manner, taking into account their vulnerability and the injustices they have faced.

The funding of asylum centers on the islands of the Aegean and the absence of asylum processing centers in the regions reinforce the 'trafficking' of those seeking international protection, compelling asylum seekers to cross maritime borders to apply for asylum on the islands, thereby putting their lives at risk. It is pertinent to acknowledge the ongoing allocation of funding toward asylum center structures. A notable illustration of this is the emergence of new asylum center facilities, termed Closed Controlled Structures, presently operational across the Greek islands. Notably, this development contrasts with the preferences expressed by the predominant local actors involved, as evidenced by the narratives gathered in this research. For narratives falling within the scope of 'impartiality', the solution is not the funding of 'detention' centers but ensuring the safe relocation of asylum seekers to their destination countries. The narrative emphasizes the obligation to put an end to the existence of asylum centers on the islands of the Aegean, not by prioritizing the local island community, but by protecting the rights of refugees. In this context, the solution would be to have asylum applications processed in countries that can halt the 'trafficking' of people. This would also reduce drownings in the Mediterranean. Moreover, an issue that primarily concerned the international press and much less the local discourse is the pushback of people who had reached the borders of the islands with the intention of seeking asylum. In the narratives of local actors who participated in the research interviews, this specific scandal is explicitly mentioned or in the form of an exploratory open question, only by 6 out of a sample of 28 interviewees.

An open question arising from this research is who ultimately has the (moral) responsibility to mitigate the challenges related to asylum centers. Some narratives emphasize the obligation of local actors to strengthen collectivity and solidarity toward asylum seekers, while in different narratives, the solution lies in the nonexistence of asylum centers. From the moment asylum seekers arrive on the islands of the Aegean, according to the narratives of local actors, the imposition of the 'geographical restriction' on the islands and the waiting in these centers until the lengthy asylum application process is completed lead to a blatant violation of human rights. Asylum seekers and the residents of the islands become the 'victims' of policies adopted by higher levels of governance, while human rights seem to have failed to put an end to the appalling conditions prevailing in the Aegean islands and their territorial waters. Europe has shifted the center of gravity to the Aegean islands by imposing the 'geographical restriction' on the islands, enforcing agreements such as the EU–Turkey Agreement and following the 'externalization of migration policy', which involves preventing and/or slowing down the acceptance of refugees by European countries. According to the narratives of local actors, during the period from 2015 to early 2021, asylum seekers were isolated on the islands, living for a period under conditions of humiliating treatment. Simultaneously, the residents of the islands serve as witnesses to these circumstances. Some among them experience a dual sense of culpability and victimization, while others perceive refugees as culpable. Alternatively, there are those who express solidarity with refugees through active engagement in solidarity actions.

I maintain that while the solidarity initiatives of local entities are crucial, the responsibility for refugee support cannot be solely theirs. Municipal authorities, as leaders, should take a more proactive stance in addressing refugee issues, advocating for increased involvement and fostering international cooperation among municipalities. Similar to the initiatives for global collaboration among nations, there is a clear need for international cooperation among municipal authorities facing similar challenges with refugees. These concerted efforts are imperative in fostering the glocalization of human rights principles at the grassroots level, thus ensuring that the foundational values of dignity and protection are not merely abstract concepts but tangible realities within local communities. By prioritizing local allocation and implementation, human rights become ingrained in the fabric of everyday life, resonating with the lived experiences of individuals in diverse socio-cultural contexts. This glocalization fosters a deeper sense of ownership and engagement with human rights principles, making them more meaningful and effective in safeguarding the rights and freedoms of all individuals, especially those in need, within their respective communities. Therefore, while the universality of human rights remains paramount, it is through their localization that human rights truly come to fruition, enriching the human experience and fostering a more just and equitable society, through the deliberate backing of local authorities.

Furthermore, I suggest that further investigation is crucial concerning the Closed Controlled Centers established on islands for asylum seekers, especially in light of the prevalent opposition from the majority of the local community, as indicated by the findings of this research and the conclusions drawn in this book. These 'all-inclusive' centers, recently replacing the RICs, are designed to accommodate asylum seekers during the processing of their asylum claims. However, this book shows that their implementation has sparked contentious debates within the local populace, with concerns ranging from human rights violations and socio-economic impacts to cultural integration and environmental sustainability. Additionally, it is my contention that in narratives describing failed attempts to prevent the creation of new Closed Controlled Structures on the islands to avoid new rights violations, the paradoxical functioning of rights is highlighted. This paradox suggests that, in order to activate a mechanism to safeguard human rights, their violation must precede. Understanding the nuanced dynamics between the establishment of such centers and the sentiments of the local community is crucial for crafting effective and sustainable refugee policies that respect human rights, including the 'vernacularization' of human rights discourse to better resonate with diverse localities. Additionally, exploring alternative approaches that address both humanitarian obligations and local concerns is essential for fostering constructive dialogue and achieving greater societal cohesion in these host communities.

Therefore, comprehensive research efforts are necessary to navigate these complex issues and inform evidence-based policymaking that balances humanitarian imperatives and human rights principles and norms with local realities, respecting the legal provisions stemming from human rights conventions. Nevertheless, in addition to the legal obligations enshrined in the Universal Declaration of Human Rights (UDHR), the 1951 Geneva Convention, the ECHR and EU Directives, the EU has a moral obligation to abolish the 'geographical restriction' of asylum seekers on the Aegean islands, cease deportations to 'safe third countries' such as Turkey, end pushbacks and accept refugees proportionally across EU countries. Seeking an answer, I would suggest considering the following analogy. Seeking an answer, I suggest that we should consider our current circumstances as largely the result of brute luck. In the same vein, I believe that the notion of random justice, including a lottery or random draw, does not solve problems but may instead perpetuate inequalities stemming from the same source: brute luck. Both egalitarian liberalism and global liberalism provide strong arguments for realizing the 'vernacularization' of rights. It is crucial to acknowledge that a single alternative (political) decision could have led us to an entirely different existence—across various regions and cultures, among different individuals, with different lives, and distinct loved ones. No one leaves their homeland without a compelling reason, and equally, no one deserves to be forced from their birthplace due to sheer brute luck.

Bibliography

Amin, Ash and Thrift, Nigel (2016). *Seeing like a city*. Cambridge, MA; Malden, MA: Polity Press.

Anderson, Elizabeth (1999). 'What is the point of equality?', *Ethics*, 109 (2), pp. 287–337.

Anderson, Elizabeth (2010). 'The fundamental disagreement between luck egalitarians and relational egalitarians', *Canadian Journal of Philosophy*, 40 (1), pp. 1–23.

Arendt, Hannah (2018). *The human condition.* 2nd edn. Chicago, IL: University of Chicago Press.

Arneson, Richard J. (2000). 'Luck egalitarianism and prioritarianism', *Ethics*, 110 (2), pp. 339–349.

Bast, Jürgen; von Harbou, Frederik and Wessels, Janna (2022). *Human rights challenges to European migration policy: The REMAP study*. Baden-Baden: Nomos and Hart Publishing.

Baumgärtel, Moritz and Oomen, Barbara (2019). 'Pulling human rights back in? Local authorities, international law and the reception of undocumented migrants', *The Journal of Legal Pluralism and Unofficial Law*, 51 (2), pp. 172–191.

Betts, Alexander (2009). *Forced migration and global politics*. Chichester; Malden, MA: Wiley-Blackwell.

Boswell, Christina (2005). *The ethics of refugee policy*. Aldershot, Burlington: Ashgate.

Cabrera, Luis (2009). 'An archaeology of borders: Qualitative political theory as a tool in addressing moral distance', *Journal of Global Ethics*, 5 (2), pp. 109–123.

Çaglar, Ayse and Glick Schiller, Nina (2018). *Migrants and city-making: Dispossession, displacement and urban regeneration*. Durham: Duke University Press.

Carens, Joseph (1992a). 'Migration and morality: A liberal egalitarian perspective'. In Barry, Ben and Goodin, Roy (eds.), *Free movement: Ethical issues in the transnational migration of people and money* (25–47). Hemel Hempstead: Harvester Wheatsheaf.

Carens, Joseph (1992b). 'Refugees and the limits of obligations', *Public Affairs Quarterly*, 6 (1), pp. 31–44.

Carens, Joseph (2013). *The ethics of immigration*. Oxford: Oxford University Press.

Cole, Philip (2000). *Philosophies of exclusion: Liberal political theory and immigration*. Edinburgh: Edinburgh University Press.

Connolly, William E. (2005). Pluralism. Durham, NC: Duke University Press.

Ciliberto, Giulia (2021). 'A brand-new exclusionary clause to the prohibition of collective expulsion of aliens: The applicant's own conduct in N.D. and N.T. v Spain', *Human Rights Law Review*, 21 (1), pp. 203–220.

Cohen, Gerald Allan (1986). 'Self-ownership, world-ownership and equality'. In Lucash, Frank S. (ed.), *Justice and equality here and now* (108–135). Ithaca, NY: Cornell University Press.

Darling, Jonathan (2009). 'A city of sanctuary: The relational re-imagining of Sheffield's asylum politics', *Transactions of the Institute of British Geographers*, 35 (1), pp. 125–140.

Darling, Jonathan (2016). 'Defying the demand to go home: From human rights cities to the urbanisation of human rights'. In Oomen, Barbara; Davis, Martha F and Grigolo, Michele (eds.), *Global urban justice: The rise of human rights cities* (155–177). Cambridge: Cambridge University Press.

de Feyter, Koen; Parmentier, Stephan; Timmerman, Christiane and Ulrich, George (eds.) (2011). *The local relevance of human rights*. Cambridge: Cambridge University Press.

Del Sarto, Raffaella A. (2010). 'Borderlands: The Middle East and North Africa as the EU's southern buffer zone'. In Bechev, Dimitar and Nicolaïdis, Kalypso (eds.), *Mediterranean frontiers: Borders, conflicts and memory in a transnational world* (149–165). London, New York: Tauris Academic Studies.

de Shalit, Avner (2018). *Cities and immigration: Political and moral dilemmas in the new era of migration*. Oxford: Oxford University Press.

Dimitriadi, Angeliki (2017). 'Governing irregular migration at the margins of Europe. The case of hotspots on the Greek islands', *Etnografia e ricerca qualitativa*, 10 (1), pp. 75–95.

Dummett, Ann (1992). 'The transnational migration of people seen from within a natural law tradition'. In Barry, Brian and Goodin, Robert E. (eds.), *Free movement: Ethical issues in the transnational migration of people and money* (169–180). University Park: Pennsylvania State University Press.

Dummett, Michael (2001). *On immigration and refugees*. London and New York: Routledge.

Dworkin, Ronald (1978). *Taking rights seriously*. 2nd edn. Cambridge, MA: Harvard University Press.

Dworkin, Ronald (1984). 'Rights as trumps'. In Waldron, Jeremy (ed.), *Theories of rights*. 1st edn. (153–167). Oxford: Oxford University Press.

Dworkin, Ronald (1992). *Phileleftherismos*, trans.: Filimon Pionidis, Thessaliki: Sakkoula. (Dworkin, Ronald. Φιλελευθερισμός, trans.: Φιλήμων Παιονίδης, Θεσσαλονίκη: Σάκκουλα.

Fernández-Wulff, Paula (2023). 'Beyond minimum protection: The politics of housing rights in the city'. In Nijman, Janne; Oomen, Barbara; Durmuş, Elif; Miellet, Sara and Roodenburg, Lisa (eds.), *Urban politics of human rights* (120–138). New York: Routledge.

Frankenberg, Günter (2014). 'Human rights and the belief in a just world', *International Journal of Constitutional Law*, 12 (1), pp. 35–60.

Freistein, Katja; Gadinger, Frank and Unrau, Christine (2020). From the global to the everyday: Anti-globalization metaphors in Trump's and Salvini's political language. Global Cooperation Research Papers 24. Duisburg: Käte Hamburger Kolleg/Centre for Global Cooperation Research (KHK/GCR21).

Gadinger, Frank; Smith Ochoa, Christopher and Yildiz, Taylan (2019). 'Resistance or thuggery? Political narratives of urban riots', Narrative Culture, 6 (1), pp. 88–111.

Gammeltoft-Hansen, Thomas (2014). 'International refugee law and refugee policy: The case of deterrence policies', *Journal of Refugee Studies*, 27 (4), pp. 574–595.

Gibney, Matthew J. (2004). *The ethics and politics of asylum: Liberal democracy and the response to refugees*, New York: Cambridge University Press.

Goodale, Mark (2007). 'Locating rights, envisioning law between the global and the local'. In Merry, Sally Engle and Goodale, Mark (eds.), *The practice of human rights tracking law between the global and the local* (5–57). Cambridge: Cambridge University Press.

Goodale, Mark (2022). *Reinventing human rights*. Redwood City, CA: Stanford University Press.

Goodwin-Gill, Guy S. and Mcadam, Jane (2007). *The refugee in international law*. Oxford: Oxford University Press.

Grigolo, Michele (2019). *The human rights city: New York, San* Fransisco, *Barcelona*. London: Routledge.

Goodwin-Gill, G. (1999) 'Refugee Identity and Protection's Fading Prospects'. In Nicholson, F. and Twomey, P. (eds) *Refugee Rights and Realities: Evolving International Concepts and Regimes*. Cambridge: Cambridge University Press.

Hardin, Garrett (1968). 'The trategy of the commons'. *Science* 162 (3859), pp. 1243–1248.

Haus, Michael (2018). 'Equality beyond Liberal Egalitarianism: Walzer's Contribution to the Theory of Justice'. In Knoll, Manuel; Snyder, Stephen and Simsek, Nurdane (eds.), *New perspectives on distributive justice* (71–79). Berlin/Boston: De Gruyter.

Hatziprokopiou, Panos; Frangopoulos, Yannis and Montagna, Nicola (2016). 'Migration and the city', *City*, 20 (1), pp. 52–60.

Heinelt, Hubert and Terizakis, Georgios (2020). 'Innovative cities: How to explain differences between cities? An answer based on an interpretive approach', *Urban Research & Practice* 14 (2), pp. 1–15.

Hlepas, Nikos-Komninos and Koliastasis, Panos (2021). Synthikes topikon kainotomion: H simasia ton epikoinoniakon michanismon kai ton topikon afigimaton. Athens: Papazisis. (Χλέπας, Νίκος – Κομνηνός και Κολιαστάσης, Πάνος, Συνθήκες τοπικών καινοτομιών: Η σημασία των επικοινωνιακών μηχανισμών και των τοπικών αφηγημάτων, Αθήνα: Παπαζήσης).

Honderich, Ted (2005). Conservatism: Burke, Nozick, Bush, Blair?. London: Pluto Press.

Hurley, Susan L. (2005). *Justice, luck and knowledge*. Cambridge, MA: Harvard University Press.

Jeandesboz, Julien and Pallister-Wilkins, Polly (2014). 'Crisis, enforcement and control at the EU borders'. In Anna Lindley (ed.), *Crisis and migration: Critical perspectives* (115–135). London: Routledge.

Jones, Martin (2013). 'The governance question: The UNHCR, the Refugee Convention and the international refugee regime'. In Simeon, James C. (ed.), *The UNHCR and the supervision of international refugee law* (75–96) Cambridge: Cambridge University Press.

Knight, Carl (2005). 'In defence of Luck Egalitarianism', Res Publica 11 (1), pp. 55–73.

Knight, Carl (2013). 'Luck Egalitarianism', *Philosophy Compass* 8 (10), pp. 924–934.

Kolliniati, Maria-Artemis (2019). *Human rights and positive obligations to healthcare: Reading the European convention on human rights through Joseph Raz's theory of rights*. Baden-Baden: Nomos.

Kolliniati, Maria-Artemis (2022). *Ta Anthropina Dikaiomata se Dokimasia: Afigiseis gia ta Kentra Ypodoxis kai Tautopoiisis se Pente Ellinika Nisia*. Athens: Gutenberg. (Κολλινιάτη, Μαρία-Άρτεμις. Τα Ανθρώπινα Δικαιώματα σε Δοκιμασία: Αφηγήσεις για τα Κέντρα Υποδοχής και Ταυτοποίησης σε Πέντε Ελληνικά Νησιά. Αθήνα: Gutenberg, 2022).

Kotzur, Markus; Moya, David; Sözen, Ülkü Sezgi and Romano, Andrea (2020). *The external dimension of EU migration and asylum policies: Border management, human rights and development policies in the Mediterranean area*. Baden-Baden: Nomos.

Kyilah, Terry (2021). 'The EU-Turkey deal, five years on: A frayed and controversial but enduring blueprint', Migration Policy Institute, Available at: https://www.migrationpolicy.org/article/eu-turkey-deal-five-years-on (Accessed: 26 January 2024).

Kymlicka, Will (2002). Contemporary *political philosophy*. Oxford: Oxford University Press.

Levitt, Peggy and Merry, Sally (2009). 'Vernacularization on the ground: Local uses of global women's rights in Peru, China, India and the United States', *Global Networks*, 9 (4), pp. 441–461.

Lippert-Rasmussen, K. (2001). 'Egalitarianism, option luck and responsibility', *Ethics*, 111 (3), pp. 548–579.

Lippert-Rasmussen, Kasper (2012). 'Democratic egalitarianism versus luck egalitarianism: What is at stake?', *Philosophical Topics*, 40 (1), pp. 117–134.

MacIntyre, Alasdair (2007). *After virtue: A study in moral theory*. 3rd edn. Notre Dame, IN: University of Notre Dame Press.

Magnusson, Warren (2011). *Politics of urbanism: Seeing like a city*. London, New York: Routledge.

Mann, Itamar (2017). *Humanity at the sea: Maritime migration and the foundations of international law*. Oxford: Oxford University Press.

Mantel, Sussane (2019). 'Not duties but needs. Rethinking Refugeehood', *Journal of Ethics and Social Philosophy* 15 (2), pp. 91–120.

McCrudden, Christopher (2006). 'Legal research and the social sciences', *Law Quarterly Review*, 122, pp. 632–650.

Merry, Sally Engle (2006). 'Transnational human rights and local activism: Mapping the middle', *American Anthropologist*, 108 (1), pp. 38–51.

Merry, Sally Engle and Levitt, Peggy (2017). 'The vernacularisation of women's human rights'. In Hopgood, Stephen; Snyder, Jack and Vinjamuri, Leslie (eds.), *Human rights futures* (213–236). Cambridge: Cambridge University Press.

Miellet, Sarra (2019). 'Human rights encounters in small places: The contestation of human rights responsibilities in three Dutch municipalities', *The Journal of Legal Pluralism and Unofficial Law*, 51 (2), pp. 213–232.

Ministry of Migration and Asylum. Receprion and *I*dentification Centers (R.I.C) & Closed Controlled Access Centers (C.C.A.C.). Available at: https://migration.gov.gr/en/ris/perifereiakes-monades/kyt-domes/ (Accessed: 15 April 2024).

Nozick, Robert (1974). *Anarchy, state and utopia*, Oxford UK, Cambridge USA: Blackwell.

Ochoa, Christopher-Smith; Gadinger, Frank and Yildiz, Taylan (2020). 'Surveillance under dispute: Conceptualising narrative legitimation politics', *European Journal of International Security*, 6 (2), pp. 210–232.

Oomen, Barbara and van den Berg, Esther (2014). 'Human rights cities: Urban actors as pragmatic idealistic human rights users', *Human Rights & International Legal Discourse*, 8 (2), pp. 160–185.

Oomen, Barbara (2015). 'Where law and politics meet – Looking at human rights law through the lens of legitimacy', *Netherlands Quarterly of Human Rights*, 33 (4), pp. 506–516.

Oomen, Barbara; Davis, Martha F. and Grigolo, Michele (eds.) (2016). *Global urban justice: The rise of human rights cities*. Cambridge: Cambridge University Press.

Oomen, Barbara and Baumgärtel, Moritz (2018). 'Frontier cities: The rise of local authorities as an opportunity for international human rights law', *The European Journal of International Law*, 29 (2), pp. 607–630.

Oomen, Barbara and Durmus, Elif (2019). 'Cities and plural understanding of human rights: Agents, actors, arenas', *The Journal of Legal Pluralism and Unofficial Law*, 51 (2), pp. 141–150.

Papoutsi, Anna; Painter, Joe; Papada, Evie and Vradis, Antonis (2019). 'The EC hotspot approach in Greece: Creating liminal EU territory', *Journal of Ethnic and Migration Studies*, 45 (2), pp. 1–13.

Patterson, Molly and Monroe, Kristen Renwick (1998). 'Narrative in political science', *Annual Review of Political Science*, 1 (1), pp. 315–331.

Pellet, Alain (2000). 'Human rightism and international law', *Italian Yearbook of International Law*, 10 (1), pp. 3–16.

Politis, George N. (ed.) (2021). Roger Scruton: Fotizontas ton Elefanta sto Domatio. Athens: Papazisis. (Πολίτης, Γιώργος Ν. (επ.). Roger Scruton: Φωτίζοντας τον Ελέφαντα στο Δωμάτιο. Αθήνα: Παπαζήσης, 2021).

Ponzo, Irene (2022). 'Reforms of asylum seekers' reception during the 2010s: Driving factors and multilevel governance arrangements'. In Caponio, Tiziana and Ponzo, Irene (eds.), *Coping with migrants and refugees multilevel governance across the EU* (38–67). London and New York: Routledge.

Poppelaars, Caelesta and Scholten, Peter (2008). 'Two worlds apart: The divergence of national and local immigrant integration policies in the Netherlands', *Administration & Society*, 40 (4), pp. 335–357.

Rawls, John (1999). *A theory of justice*. rev. edn. Cambridge, MA: Harvard University Press.

Rawls, John (2002). *The law of peoples*. Cambridge, MA: Harvard University Press.

Reed, Kristin and Padskocimaite, Ausra (2012). *The right toolkit: Applying research methods in the service of human rights*. Berkley: Human Rights Center University of California, Berkeley School of Law.

Resnik, Judith (2007). 'Foreign as domestic affairs: Rethinking horizontal federalism and foreign affairs preemption in light of translocal internationalism', *Emory Law Journal*, 57 (1), pp. 31–92.

Roy, Ananya (2019). 'The city in the age of Trumpism: From sanctuary to abolition', *Environment and Planning D: Society and Space*, 37 (5), pp. 761–778.

Saibih, Junaedi (2019). 'Using narrative theory on analysis of law and human rights: Searching truth on Tanjung Priok's incident in Indonesia', *Advances in Economics, Business and Management Research*, 130, pp. 273–284.

Sandel, Michael J. (ed.) (1984). *Liberalism and its critics: Readings in social and political theory*. New York: New York University Press.

Sandel, Michael J. (1998). *Liberalism and the limits of justice*. 2nd edn. Cambridge: Cambridge University Press.

Sanyal, Romola (2012). 'Refugees and the city: An urban discussion', *Geography Compass*, 6 (11), pp. 633–644.

Sabchev, Tihomir (2021a). 'Against all odds: Thessaloniki's local policy activism in the reception and integration of forced migrants', *Journal of Ethnic and Migration Studies*, 47 (7), pp. 1435–1454.

Sabchev, Tihomir (2021b). *Local authorities, human rights and the reception and integration of forced migrants in Greece and Italy*. Utrecht: Utrecht University.

Sabchev, Tihomir (2022). 'Potential and limits of municipal solidarity with refugees: A case study of the Greek island of Tilos', *Journal of Immigrant & Refugee Studies*, 22 (3), pp. 614–631.

Saunders, Doug (2010). *Arrival city: How the largest migration in history is reshaping our world*. London: William Heinemann.

Schaffer, Kay and Smith, Sidonie (2004). *Human rights and narrated lives: The ethics of recognition*. New York: Palgrave Macmillan.

Segarra, Helena (2023). 'Dismantling the reception of asylum seekers: Hungary's illiberal asylum policies and EU responses', *East European Politics*, 40 (1), pp. 43–63.

Shapiro, Danny (2013). 'Does Ronald Dworkin take rights seriously?', *Canadian Journal of Philosophy*, 12 (3), pp. 417–434.

Spathopoulou, Aila (2022). *Bordering and governmentality around the Greek islands*. London: Palgrave Macmillan.

Stürner, Janina and Bendel, Petra (2019). 'The two-way glocalisation of human rights or: How cities become international agents in migration governance', *Peace Human Rights Governance*, 3 (2), pp. 215–240.

Talisse, Robert (2000). *On rawls: A theory of justice and justification*. Belmont, CA: Wadsworth Thomson Learning.

Tan, Kok-Chor (2008). 'A defense of luck egalitarianism', *The Journal of Philosophy*, 105 (11), pp. 665–690.

Taubenböck, Hannes; Kraff, Nicolas-Johannes and Wurm, Michael (2018). 'The morphology of the arrival city. A global categorization based on literature surveys and remotely sensed data', *Applied Geography*, 92, pp. 150–167.

Taylor, Charles (2001). *Sources of the self: The making of the modern identity*. 10th edn. Cambridge, MA: Harvard University Press.

Trubeta, Sevasti (2015). 'Rights in the grey area: Undocumented border crossers on Lesvos', *Race & Class*, 56 (4), pp. 56–72.

Turner, Marianne and Fozdar, Farida (2010). 'Dependency, partiality and the generation of research questions in refugee education', *Issues in Educational Research* 20 (2), pp. 183–197.

Tsavdaroglou, Charalampos (2019). 'Reimagining a transnational right to the city: No border actions and commoning practices in Thessaloniki', *Cogitatio*, 7 (2), pp. 219–229.

Valenta, Marko; Lønning, Moa-Nyamwathi; Jakobsen, Jo and Zuparic-Iljic, Drago (2019). 'European asylum policies and the stranded asylum seekers in Southeastern Europe', *Journal of Refugee Studies*, 32 (Special Issue 1), pp. 162–171.

Vandvik, Bjarte (2008). 'Extraterritorial border controls and responsibility: A view from ECRE', *Amsterdam Law Forum*, 1 (1), pp. 27–36.

Voigt, Kristin (2018). 'Relational equality and the expressive dimension of State Action', *Social Theory and Practice*, 44 (3), pp. 437–467.

Walzer, Michael (1983). *Spheres of justice: A defence of pluralism and equality*. New York: Basic Books.

Wellman, Christopher-Heath and Cole, Phillip (2011). *Debating the ethics of immigration: Is there a right to exclude?* Oxford: Oxford University Press.

Wolff, Robert-Paul (1977). *Understanding rawls: A reconstruction and critique of a theory of justice*. Princeton, NJ: Princeton University Press.

Ziebritzki, Catharina (2018). 'Implementation of the EU-Turkey Statement: EU Hotspots and restriction of asylum seekers' freedom of movement', EU Migration Law Blog, 22 June. Available at: https://eumigrationlawblog.eu/implementation-of-the-eu-turkey-statement-eu-hotspots-and-restriction-of-asylum-seekers-freedom-of-movement/ (Accessed: 2 February 2024).

Ziebritzki, Catharina (2020). 'Refugee Camps at EU External Borders, the Question of the Union's Responsibility and the Potential of EU Public Liability Law', Verfassungsblog, 5 February. Available at: https://verfassungsblog.de/refugee-camps-at-eu-external-borders-the-question-of-the-unions-responsibility-and-the-potential-of-eu-public-liability-law/ (Accessed: 2 February 2024).

Resolutions, EU legal acts, agreements and other sources

Communication to the ICC (2019). Communication to the Office of the Prosecutor of the International Criminal Court Pursuant to the Article 15 of the Rome Statute, EU Migration Policies in the Central Mediterranean and Libya (2014–2019).

Congress of Local and Regional Authorities, CG34,10 final. "Promoting human rights at local and regional level," Monitoring Committee (27 March 2018).

Convention Relating to the Status of Refugees (adopten on the 28th of July 1951; entry into force on the 22nd of April 1954) 189 UNTS 137 (Refugee Convention).

Council of Europe (1950). *European Convention for the Protection of Human Rights and Fundamental Freedoms, as amended by Protocols Nos. 11 and 14, supplemented by Protocols Nos. 1, 4, 6, 7, 12 and 13*, 4. Strasbourg.

Council of Europe (2019). *Resolution 2299: Pushback policies and practice in Council of Europe member States*. Strasbourg: Parliamentary Assembly.

Council of Europe (2022). *Pushed beyond the limits. Urgent action needed to stop push-backs at Europe's borders*. Strabourg: Commissioner for Human Rights.

De Blasio, Bill; Hidalgo, Anne and Khan, Sadiq (2016). 'Our immigrants, our strength', *New York Times*, 20 September. Available at: https://www.nytimes.com/2016/09/20/opinion/our-immigrants-our-strength.html (Accessed: 25 January 2024).

Directive 2011/95/EU (EU Qualification Directive) of the European Parliament and of the Council of 13 December 2011 on standards for the qualification of third-country nationals or stateless persons as beneficiaries of international protection, for a uniform status for refugees or for persons eligible for subsidiary protection and for the content of the protection granted.

Directive 2013/32/EU of the European Parliament and of the Council of 26 June 2013 on common procedures for granting and withdrawing international protection.

Dublin Convention – Convention determining the State responsible for examining applications for asylum lodged in one of the Member States of the European Communities (97/C 254/01). Date of end of validity: 16/03/2003.

Dumbrava, C. (2020). Screening of third-country nationals at the EU's external borders. EPRS, European Parliament, November 2020.

European Center for Constitutional and Human Rights (ECCHR). Dossier: Migration, June 2020.

European Commission (2015a). *European Agenda on Migration COM/2015/0240, COM (2015)* 240, 13 May 2015.

European Commission (2015b). EU-Turkey Joint Action Plan, Fact sheet, MEMO/15/5860, November 2015.

European Commission (2015c). Commission presents a recommendation for a Voluntary Humanitarian Admission Scheme with Turkey for refugees from Syria, Press release, IP/15/6330, December 2015.

European Council (2016). EU-Turkey Statement, Press release, 144/16, 18 March 2016.

European Economic and Social Committee (2021). «Η εξωτερική διάσταση της μετανάστευσης πρέπει να ενσωματωθεί στην εξωτερική πολιτική της ΕΕ», EESC -2021-04027-00-00-CP.

European Parliament (2016). Resolution of 14 April 2016 on the 2015 Report on Turkey (2015/2898 (RSP)).

European Parliament (2016). 'Study on the frontline: The hotspot approach to managing exceptional migratory flows'. In Neville, Darren, Sy, Sarah and Rigon, Amalia (eds.), *Policy department for citizen's rights and constitutional affairs*. Brussels: Policy Department for Citizen's Rights and Constitutional Affairs.

European Parliament (2021). Pushbacks at the EU's external borders, Briefing. Brussels: EPRS - European Parliamentary Research Service.

European Union Agency for Fundamental Rights (2020). Migration: Fundamental rights issues at land borders.

European Union. Convention Determining the State Responsible for Examining Applications for Asylum lodged in one of the Member States of the European Communities (Dublin Convention), 15 June 1990, Official Journal C 254, 19/08/1997 p. 0001 – 0012. [No longer in force, Date of end of validity: 16/03/2003; Replaced by Council Regulation (EC) No 343/2003 of 18 February 2003 establishing the criteria and mechanisms for determining the Member State responsible for examining an asylum application lodged in one of the Member States by a third-country national]

European Union: Council of the European Union. Regulation (EU) No 604/2013 of the European Parliament and of the Council of 26 June 2013 establishing the criteria and mechanisms for determining the Member State responsible for examining an application for international protection lodged in one of the Member States by a third-country national or a stateless person, 26 June 2013, OJ L. 180/31-180/59; 29.6.2013, (EU)No 604/2013.

Greek Law 4375/2016 (A'51/3.4.2016). "On the organization and operation of the Asylum Service, the Appeals Authority, the Reception and Identification Service, the establishment of the General Secretariat for Reception, the transposition into Greek legislation of the provisions of Directive 2013/32/EC "on common procedures for granting and withdrawing the status of international protection (recast)" (L 180/29.6.2013), provisions on the employment of beneficiaries of international protection and other provisions."

Greek Law 4619/2019 (A' 122/16.07.2019). Criminal Code.

Greek Law 4636/2019 (A' 169/01.11.2019). On International Protection and other provisions.

Greek Law 4825/2021 (A' 157/4.9.2021). "Reform of deportation and return procedures of third-country nationals, attracting investors and digital nomads, issues of residence permits and procedures for granting international protection, provisions of the Ministry of Migration and Asylum and the Ministry of Citizen Protection and other urgent provisions."

Greek Law 4939/2022 (Government Gazette 111/A/10.6.2022). "Ratification of a Code of Legislation on the reception, international protection of third country citizens and stateless persons and temporary protection in the event of a mass influx of displaced foreigners."

Greek Ministerial Decision No. 2969/2015 (Government Gazette 2602/B/2.12.2015). 'Establishment of First Reception Centers and Temporary Accommodation Facilities for asylum seekers and vulnerable groups of third-country nationals'.

Greek Ministerial Decision No. 3063/2020. 'Register of Greek and Foreign Non-Governmental Organizations (NGOs)' and the 'Register of Members of Non-Governmental Organizations (NGOs)'.

Greek Ministerial Decision No. 10616/2020. 'Register of Greek and Foreign Non-Governmental Organizations (NGOs)' and the 'Register of Members of Non-Governmental Organizations (NGOs)'.

Hellenic Statistical Authority (ELSTAT), Census 2011.

Radjenovic A. *Reforming asylum and migration management*. EPRS, European Parliament, October 2020.

Radjenovic A. *Search and rescue in the Mediterranean*. EPRS, European Parliament, January 2021.

Rankin, Jennifer. (2022). 'EU censures border agency after reports of human rights abuses in Greece.' *The Guardian*, 04/05/22.

Regulation (EU) No 604/2013 (or Dublin III Regulation) of the European Parliament and of the Council of 26 June 2013 establishing the criteria and mechanisms for determining the Member State responsible for examining an application for international protection lodged in one of the Member States by a third-country national or a stateless person (recast).

'Regulation (EU) 2016/399 of the European Parliament and of the Council of 9 March 2016 on a Union Code on the rules governing the movement of persons across borders (Schengen Borders Code) (codification)' (2016) *Official Journal L*, 77 (1), pp. 1–52. https://data.europa.eu/eli/reg/2016/399/oj

Synigoros tou Politi, Annual Report 2020 (Συνήγορος του Πολίτη [Ombudsman] -Ανεξάρτητη Αρχή, Ετήσια Έκθεση 2020 [Annual report 2020]).

Υπουργείο Μετανάστευσης και Ασύλου, ετήσια αναφορά 12/2020 (Ετήσιο Ενημερωτικό Σημείωμα 2020), Accessed: October 2021, at: https://migration.gov.gr/statistika/

United Nations Development Programme/UNDP Oslo Governance Centre. 'A Users' Guide to Measuring Local Governance' (2009).

United Nations Human Rights. (2012). 'Human rights indicators: A Guide to Measurement and Implementation'.

United Nations General Assembly (1948). 'The Universal Declaration of Human Rights (UDHR).' New York: United Nations General Assembly.

United Nations General Assembly. Convention Relating to the Status of Refugees, 28 July 1951, United Nations, Treaty Series, vol. 189.

United Nations (1969). 'Vienna Convention on the Law of Treaties.' *Treaty Series*, vol. 1155, p. 331.

UNHCR (2021a). UNHCR warns asylum under attack at Europe's borders, urges end to pushbacks and violence against refugees, Press releases, 28 January 2021.

UNHCR (2021b). Report on means to address the human rights impact of pushbacks of migrants on land and at sea, A/HRC/47/30, 12 May 2021.

European Court of Human Rights case law

D. v. The United Kingdom (D v. UK), (Chamber), Application no. 30240/96, decision of May 2, 1997.

Othman (Abu Qatada) v United Kingdom, (Fourth Section), Application no. 8139/09, decision of January 17, 2012 /final decision on the 9th of May 2012.

ND and NT vs. Spain, (Grand Chamber), Application nos. 8675/15 και 8697/15, decision of February 13, 2020.

Appendix

Table A.1 Interviews profile summary table

Code	*Municipality*	*Date*	*Local actors*	*Language*
P1	Mytilini municipality (Lesvos)	13/11/20	Christos Vasileiou, National Director, Eurorelief Hellas	Greek
P2	East Samos municipality	18/11/20	Despina Syropoulou, Social Worker, Greek Council for Refugees (GCR), Samos Office (2020)	Greek
P3	East Samos municipality	19/11/20	Michiel Zwijnenburg, Communications and Fundraising Coordinator, Samos Volunteers	English
P4	East Samos municipality	25/11/20	Alkistis Agrafioti Chatyigianni, Lawyer, Greek Council for Refugees (GCR), Samos Office (2020)	Greek
P5	Mytilini municipality	30/11/20	Eric Verhaar, Field Operations Officer, Movement on the ground	English
P6	Leros municipality	01/12/20	NGO[a]	English
P7	Leros municipality	01/12/20	NGO[a]	English
P8	Chios municipality	03/12/20	Jenny Kalipozi, Solidarity in Chios	Greek
P9	Leros municipality	21/12/20	Anna Maria Palyvou, Coordinator of the Informal Education Center in Leros, ARSIS Leros, LEDU	Greek
P10	Cos municipality	22/12/20	Xenia Hatzidavid, Coordinator of the Informal Education Center in Cos, ARSIS Cos, KEDU	Greek
P11	East Samos municipality	22/12/20	Beatrice Azzani, Field Operations Officer Samos, Movement on the ground	English
P12	Chios municipality	14/01/21	Ermioni Frezouli, Municipal Councillor, «Chiaki Sympoliteia»	Greek

(*Continued*)

Table A.1 (Continued)

Code	*Municipality*	*Date*	*Local actors*	*Language*
P13	Chios municipality	14/01/21	Dimitris Antonoglou, Municipali Councillor, «Chiaki Sympoliteia»	Greek
P14	All five islands	21/01/21	Erasmia Roumana, Senior Protection Associate, the UN Refugee Agency (UNHCR), Greece	Greek
P15	Cos municipality	22/01/21	Kiki Makri, Municipal Councillor, «Laiki Syspirosi» Cos	Greek
P16	Leros municipality	22/01/21	Rolina Sotiriadou, Psychologist in the RIC for asylum seekers, Leros	Greek
P17	All five islands	26/01/21	Spyros Apergis, Lawyer, European Union Agency for Asylum, former member of the committees for asylum seekers claims of the Ministries of Citizen Protection, Interior and Migration Policies, between 2011–2015 and 2016–2019.	Greek
P18	Cos municipality	18/02/21	Theodosis Nikitaras, Mayor of Cos	Greek
P19	Leros municipality	23/02/21	Michalis Kolias, Mayor of Leros	Greek
P20	Chios municipality	25/02/21	Giannis Karavasilis, Municipal councillor, «Chios Brosta»	Greek
P21	East Samos municipality	08/03/21	Nikos Zacharis, Municipal councillor, «H Samos allaZEI»	Greek
P22	Leros municipality	09/03/21	Ioannis Sorokakis, Municipal councillor, «To Mellon sou Anikei»	Greek
P23	Mytilini municipality	11/03/21	Erifyli Chiotelli, Municipal councillor «Me piksida ton politi»	Greek
P24	East Samos municipality	12/03/21	Georgios Stantzos, Mayor of East Samos	Greek
P25	Mytilini municipality	26/03/21	Tasos Balis, on behalf of the mayor of Mytilini Eustratio Kyteli,	Greek
P26	Chios municipality	02/04/21	Eirini Papanastasiou, ARSIS Chios	Greek
P27	Cos municipality	08/05/21	Ioannis Fragkoulis, Administrator of RIC Cos	Greek
P28	Leros municipality	09/05/21	Filio Kyprizoglou, Administrator of RIC Leros	Greek

[a] To remain anonymous.

Index

Note: **Bold** page numbers refer to tables and page numbers followed by "n" denote endnotes.

9781032638522